Cover Artist
Brenda DiAntonis

Managing Editor
Ina Massler Levin, M.A.

Creative Director
Karen J. Goldfluss, M.S. Ed.

Art Production Manager
Kevin Barnes

Art Coordinator
Renée Christine Yates

Imaging
Leonard Swierski
Rosa C. See

Publisher
Mary D. Smith, M.S. Ed.

Document-Based Questions

for Reading Comprehension and Critical Thinking

Grade **5**

Author

Debra J. Housel, M.S. Ed.

The classroom teacher may reproduce copies of materials in this book for classroom use only. Reproduction of any part for an entire school or school system is strictly prohibited. No part of this publication may be transmitted, stored, or recorded in any form without written permission from the publisher.

Teacher Created Resources, Inc.
6421 Industry Way
Westminster, CA 92683
www.teachercreated.com
ISBN: 978-1-4206-8375-2
© 2007 Teacher Created Resources, Inc.
Made in U.S.A.

Table of Contents

About This Book

The primary goal of any reading task is comprehension. *Document-Based Questions for Reading Comprehension and Critical Thinking* uses high-interest grade-level nonfiction passages, related documents, and critical thinking assessment practice to help you develop confident readers who can demonstrate their skills on standardized tests. In addition, you will build the comprehension skills necessary for a lifetime of learning.

There are five topic areas with six or seven lessons in each. Each lesson consists of three pages: a passage, a related document, and an assessment practice page containing multiple choice, true-false-explain, and short-answer document-based questions. This gives your students practice in all of the question types used in standardized testing. The students respond to the document-based questions based on the information gleaned from the passage plus its related document. Such questions improve a student's ability to apply prior knowledge, integrate information, and transfer knowledge to a new situation.

Readability

These passages have a 5.0–5.9 reading level based on the Flesch-Kincaid Readability Formula. This formula, built into *Microsoft® Word™*, determines readability by calculating the number of words, syllables, and sentences. Average readability was determined for each of the five topic areas. The topics are presented in order of increasing difficulty.

The documents are not leveled. Many of them are historical pieces and therefore replicated with the exact wording. Some terminology may be challenging, but your students can handle difficult words within the context given.

Preparing Students to Read Nonfiction Text

One of the best ways to prepare students to read expository text is to read a short selection aloud to them daily. Reading expository text aloud is critical to developing your students' ability to read it themselves. Since making predictions is another way to make students tap into their prior knowledge, read the beginning of a passage, then stop, and ask them to predict what might occur next. Do this at several points throughout your reading of the text. By doing this, over time you will find that your students' ability to make accurate predictions increases.

Your questions will help students, especially struggling readers, focus on what's important in a text. Also, remember the significance of wait time. Research has shown that the amount of time an educator waits for a student to answer after posing a question has a critical effect on learning. So after you ask a student a question, silently count to five (ten if you have a student who really struggles to put his or her thoughts into words) before giving any additional prompts or redirecting the question to another student.

Talking about nonfiction concepts is also important. Remember, however, that discussion can never replace reading aloud because people rarely speak using the vocabulary and complex sentence structures of written language.

Applying Bloom's Taxonomy

The questions on the assessment practice pages in *Document-Based Questions for Reading Comprehension and Critical Thinking* assess all levels of learning in Bloom's Taxonomy. Benjamin Bloom devised this six-level classification system for comprehension questions. The questions on each assessment practice passage are always presented in this order. They progress from easiest to most challenging.

- **Level 1: Knowledge**—Students recall information or can find requested information in an article. They recognize dates, events, places, people, and main ideas.
- **Level 2: Comprehension**—Students understand information. This means that they can find information that is stated in a different way than the question. It also means students can rephrase or restate information in their own words.
- **Level 3: Application**—Students apply their knowledge to a specific situation. They may be asked to do something new with the knowledge.
- **Level 4: Analysis**—Students break things into their component parts and examine those parts. They notice patterns in information.
- **Level 5: Synthesis**—Students do something new with the information. They integrate knowledge and create new ideas. They generalize, predict, plan, and draw conclusions.
- **Level 6: Evaluation**—Students make judgments and assess value. They form an opinion and defend it. They can also understand another person's viewpoint.

These skills are essential to keep in mind when teaching comprehension to ensure that your students practice the higher levels of thinking. Use this classification to form your own questions whenever your students read or listen to material.

Assessment Practice Pages

Teach your students to read the passage and its related document before answering any of the questions on the assessment practice page. Armed with this information, your students can more rapidly and accurately answer each question.

Multiple Choice Questions

The first three questions are multiple choice. Based solely on the information given in the passage, they cover the knowledge, comprehension, and application levels of Bloom's taxonomy.

For these questions, demonstrate your own thought process by doing a "think aloud" to figure out an answer. Tell your students your thoughts as they come to you. For example, suppose the question was: "In Yellowstone National Park, grizzly bears (a) do tricks, (b) roam free, (c) stay in cages, or (d) get caught in traps."

Tell the students all your thoughts as they occur to you:

"Well, the grizzly bears living in Yellowstone National Park are wild bears. So of course they don't do tricks. And it didn't mention that they stay in cages. They probably only do that in zoos or circuses. So I'll get rid of choices A and C. That leaves me with 'roam free' or 'get caught in traps.' Let me look back at the passage and see what it says about traps."

Applying Bloom's Taxonomy *(cont.)*

Multiple Choice Questions *(cont.)*

(Refer back to article.)

"I don't see anything about traps in the passage. And I did see that it says that in Yellowstone National Park the bears are protected and their population is increasing. That means they're safe from traps, which are dangerous. So I'm going to select (b)—roam free."

True/False—Explain Questions

The fourth question is true/false—explain. It tests the analysis level of Bloom's taxonomy. This question may require students to use information from both the passage and the document to generate an answer. Just a one- or two-sentence response is required. To respond correctly, students must not only distinguish facts from falsehoods but also explain them. This requires logical reasoning and analytical thinking. They cannot receive full credit without an adequate explanation. You must demonstrate how to write a good explanation. For example, in response to the statement: "Thomas Jefferson wrote the Gettysburg Address," the students could write, "False. Abraham Lincoln wrote the Gettysburg Address" OR "False. Thomas Jefferson wrote the Declaration of Independence." Either answer is acceptable and worth full credit.

When the statement is clearly true, the student must state that and add information. For example, in response to the statement: "Early pioneers in the Midwest had to cope with grasshopper plagues," the students should write, "True. The grasshoppers destroyed crops and even damaged buildings."

Make sure that your students know that sometimes both true and false responses can be correct. For example, in an article about rescuing Jewish children from the Warsaw Ghetto, it states how hard it was to convince the parents to let the rescue organization take away their children. It also details the methods used to get the kids past the guards (crawling through sewers, sedated babies in toolboxes). In response to the question, " During the rescue operation, the most difficult part was getting the parents to release their kids to the rescuers," some students may respond "True. Many parents did not want to let their children go. They were not sure that the children were in danger and thought that they could protect them." But others may say, "False. The hardest part was getting the kids out of the Ghetto without the Gestapo discovering what was going on."

Either response is worth full credit because it is adequately defended. This promotes critical thinking since the students must digest the information in order to take a stance.

Document-Based Questions

The remaining questions require the students to integrate the information provided in the passage with the information shown in the document. You must guide your students in understanding and responding to the document-based questions. Again, the best way to teach such skills is to demonstrate the formulation of an answer through a think aloud.

Applying Bloom's Taxonomy *(cont.)*

Short-Answer Questions

The fifth and sixth questions test the synthesis and evaluative levels of Bloom's taxonomy. Synthesis questions make your students draw conclusions based on information gleaned from both the passage and its document. Their response requires only a few sentences. Show your students how to restate the words from the question to formulate a cogent response. For example, in response to "Why were some people against the building of the Hoover Dam?" the students could write, "Some people were against the building of the Hoover Dam because it backed up a river, forming a huge lake. Historical Native American sites were flooded and animals' homes destroyed."

The final short answer question will be evaluative—the highest level of Bloom's taxonomy. This means that it is an opinion statement with no right answer. Evaluative questions demand the highest thinking and logical reasoning skills. The child must take a stance and defend it. Although there is no correct response, it is critical that the students support their opinions using facts and logic. Show them a format for the defense—by stating their opinion followed by the word "because" and a reason. For example, have a student respond to this question: "Do you think that whales should be kept in aquariums and sea parks for people to enjoy?" The student may respond, "I do not think that whales should be kept at sea parks because they are wild animals and don't want to be there. They want to be free in the ocean." Do not award full credit unless the student adequately supports his or her opinion.

Sample defenses are given for the evaluative questions, but students may present other valid opinions as well. Also, it would be most effective if you used the defenses written by the students themselves. Thus, before passing back the practice papers, make note of two children who had opposing opinions. Then, during the wrap-up discussion, call on each of these students to read his or her defense to the class. If all the children had the same conclusion, give the opposing opinion from the answer key to show them both sides of the issue. When it's obvious that a topic has generated strong opinions in your students, you can encourage your class to debate.

Practice Suggestions

Read aloud the first passage in each of the five topic areas and do its related questions with the whole class. Such group practice is essential. The more your students practice, the more competent and confident they will become. Plan to have your class do every exercise in the *Document-Based Questions for Reading Comprehension and Critical Thinking.* The activities are time-efficient so that your students can practice each week. To yield the best results, practice must begin at the start of the school year.

If you have some students who cannot read the articles independently, allow them to read with a partner, then work through the comprehension questions alone. Eventually all students must practice reading and answering the questions independently. Move to this stage as soon as possible. For the most effective practice sessions, follow these steps:

1. Have students read the text silently and answer the questions.

2. Have students exchange papers to correct each other's multiple choice section.

3. Collect all the papers to score the short answer questions.

4. Return the papers to their owners and discuss how the students determined their answers.

5. Refer to the exact wording in the passage.

6. Point out how students had to use their background knowledge to answer certain questions.

7. Discuss the document-based questions thoroughly. Do think-alouds to show how you integrated information from the passage and the document to formulate your response.

8. Discuss how a child should defend his or her stance in an evaluative short-answer question.

Scoring the Assessment Practice Pages

To generate a numeric score, follow these guidelines:

Multiple choice questions (3)	12 points each	36 points
True/False—Explain question (1)	16 points	16 points
Short-answer questions (2)	24 points each	48 points
	Total	100 points

Standardized Test Success

A key objective of *Document-Based Questions for Reading Comprehension and Critical Thinking* is to prepare your students to get the best possible scores on standardized tests. You may want to practice environmental conditions throughout the year in order to get your students used to the testing environment. For example, if your students' desks are usually together, have students move them apart whenever you practice so it won't feel strange on the test day.

A student's ability to do well on traditional standardized tests on comprehension requires these good test-taking skills. Thus, every student in your class needs instruction in test-taking skills. Even fluent readers and logical thinkers will perform better on standardized tests if you provide instruction in these areas:

- Understanding the question: Teach students to break down the question to figure out what is really being asked of them. This book will prepare them for the kinds of questions they will encounter on standardized tests.

- Concentrating on what the text says: Show students how to restrict their responses to just what is asked. When you go over the practice pages, ask your students to show where they found the correct response or inference in the text.

- Ruling out distracters in multiple choice answers: Teach students to look for the key words in a question and look for those specific words to find the information in the text. They also need to know that they may have to look for synonyms for the key words.

- Maintaining concentration: Use classroom time to practice this in advance. Reward students for maintaining concentration. Explain to them the purpose of this practice and the reason why concentration is so essential.

Students will need to use test-taking skills and strategies throughout their lives. The exercises in *Document-Based Questions for Reading Comprehension and Critical Thinking* will guide your students to become better readers and test-takers. After practicing the exercises in this book, you will be pleased with your students' comprehension performance, not only on standardized tests, but with any expository text they encounter—within the classroom and beyond its walls.

Standards and Benchmarks

Listed below are the McREL standards for Language Arts Level II (grades 3–5). All standards and benchmarks are used with permission from McREL.

Kendall, J. S., & Marzano, R. J. (2004). *Content knowledge: A compendium of standards and benchmarks for K-12 education*. Aurora, CO: Mid-continent Research for Education and Learning. Online database:

http://www.mcrel.org/standards-benchmarks/

McREL Standards are in bold. Benchmarks are in regular print. All lessons meet the following standards and benchmarks.

STANDARD 5 **Level II**	**Uses the general skills and strategies of the reading process.**
Benchmark 3	Makes, confirms, and revises simple predictions about what will be found in a text (e.g., uses prior knowledge and ideas presented in text, illustrations, titles, topic sentences, key words, and foreshadowing clues)
Benchmark 7	Understands level-appropriate reading vocabulary (e.g., synonyms, antonyms, homophones, multi-meaning words)
Benchmark 10	Understands the author's purpose (e.g., to persuade, to inform) or point of view
STANDARD 7	**Uses reading skills and strategies to understand and interpret a variety of informational texts**
Level II	
Benchmark 1	Uses reading skills and strategies to understand a variety of informational texts (e.g., textbooks, biographical sketches, letters, diaries, directions, procedures, magazines)
Benchmark 5	Summarizes and paraphrases information in texts (e.g., includes the main idea and significant supporting details of a reading selection)
Benchmark 6	Uses prior knowledge and experience to understand and respond to new information
STANDARD 1 **Level II**	**Uses the general skills and strategies of the writing process.**
Benchmark 6	Uses strategies (e.g., adapts focus, point of view, organization, form) to write for a variety of purposes (e.g., to inform, entertain, explain, describe, record ideas)
Benchmark 7	Writes expository compositions (e.g., identifies and stays on the topic; develops the topic with simple facts, details, examples, and explanations; excludes extraneous and inappropriate information; uses structures such as cause-and-effect, chronology, similarities and differences; uses several sources of information; provides a concluding statement)

The Female Moses

Born a slave on a Maryland plantation around 1820, Harriet Tubman was the sixth of 11 children. Her family lived in a one-room hut with a dirt floor and no windows. By the time she turned five, she worked in the fields. At the age of eight she cared for a white infant 24 hours a day.

Harriet discovered how brave she could be as a young teen. She saw a slave running from his owner. Runaway slaves who were caught were beaten, sometimes to death. To give him time to escape, Harriet stepped between them. The angry master threw a flat iron. It hit her in the head and almost killed her. From then on, Harriet decided that she would one day be free.

In 1844 Harriet married John Tubman, a free man, and told him of her desire to be free. He told her to forget about it. And when she told him about her plans to run away, he said he would tell her owner! One night in 1849 she did escape with three of her brothers, but the men were terrified. All four turned back. Two nights later she escaped alone to the home of a white woman who had offered her help. The woman was a member of the Underground Railroad. This was a secret network of people who helped escaping slaves reach the north. To avoid capture, Harriet hid at their homes or in barns during the day. She traveled only at night until she reached Pennsylvania.

Over the next ten years she returned 19 times to lead more than 300 slaves on the Underground Railroad. Posters offering money for her capture dead or alive appeared all over the South, but nobody caught her. She cleverly disguised herself as a man or an elderly woman.

Running away was a terrifying experience. Sometimes the people had to hide in swamps that had alligators and poisonous snakes. But once slaves started north, Harriet would not let them go back. She knew that under torture they might give up information about the Underground Railroad. That would ruin the escape route. If a runaway wanted to turn back, Harriet would point a gun at the person and say, "Go on or die." Fortunately, she never had to pull the trigger, and she never lost a single person to slave catchers. People called her Moses because she led her people out of slavery.

During the Civil War, Harriet served as a nurse and a spy for the Union Army. All the slaves were set free at the end of the war. She went to Auburn, New York. There she opened a home for sick, poor, or homeless blacks. She also worked for women's right to vote. When she was about 90 years old, she died in her sleep.

The Female Moses

WANTED
—DEAD OR ALIVE—

RUNAWAY SLAVE

$10,000 REWARD

Report Whereabouts to Local Law Authorities or Eliza Brodess, Owner

The Female Moses

1. How did Harriet get a head injury?

a. She was hit in the head with a flat iron.

b. Her master beat her after she was caught escaping.

c. She was in a battle while serving as a Union spy during the Civil War.

d. A slave catcher attacked her.

2. The Underground Railroad was

a. the main rail line connecting the North and the South.

b. a secret escape route for slaves.

c. a group of people who kidnapped others and sold them into slavery.

d. a group of people who kidnapped slaves and then smuggled them to safety.

3. What did Harriet demonstrate over and over again?

a. joy

b. anger

c. courage

d. sorrow

4. Harriet spent the last years of her life in New York state. True or False? Explain.

_____

_____

_____

5. What was the amount of money offered for Harriet's capture and why was the sum so large?

_____

_____

_____

_____

_____

6. Did Harriet do the right thing by threatening to kill any runaways who wanted to turn back? Defend your stance.

_____

_____

_____

_____

Nellie Bly, Investigative Reporter

Nellie Bly was born Elizabeth Jane Cochran in 1864. She grew up to become the first woman undercover reporter. When she was 18, Nellie wrote an anonymous letter to the editor of the *Pittsburgh Dispatch*. She responded to a sexist article the paper had printed. Her letter so impressed the editor that he ran an ad asking to meet her. He hired her. She took the pen name Nellie Bly and used it for the rest of her life. After a while, she grew restless. She wanted to write stories that brought about reform. So in September 1887, Nellie joined the staff of the *New York World*. Her first task? Be committed to the Women's Lunatic Asylum on Blackwell Island.

Courtesy of the Library of Congress, "Nellie Bly," LC-USZ62-75620

Nellie went there thinking that the people would be well-cared for. Instead she found shocking conditions. A woman could get committed to the asylum for life without proof of insanity. Nellie saw immigrants there simply because no one had met them in America and they spoke a foreign language. During her 10 grim days there, Nellie saw sane women so mistreated that they started to lose their grip on reality.

The nurses and doctors living on the island ate all the fresh fruits, vegetables, and meat. The patients had stale bread with rotten butter and weak tea. They were nearly starved. They were deliberately kept so cold that they shook most of the time. If they got sick and died, no one cared! They saw each death as making room for a new patient.

Once a week all the women in a hall took a bath in ice-cold water. The tub was filled once, and each woman dunked in it! This led to the spread of diseases and skin sores. Six combs were used on 45 women, causing head lice to spread. The "lucky" patients got to clean the place without pay, including the nurses' rooms and clothes. Others had to sit up straight for hours on benches without backs. They could not move without being punished. And the punishments were awful. Hair was yanked out by the handful. Women who cried were choked, kicked, slapped, or beaten. Others got locked in a closet. If a woman told a doctor about the mistreatment, she had her head held underwater until she almost drowned.

The editor sent a lawyer to get Nellie. She wrote about the terrible conditions. A grand jury called her to testify. The jurors asked her to go with them to the island. Although their visit was supposed to be secret, word got out. Things appeared presentable on that day. Still, the grand jury believed Nellie. It advised changes to the court. The court gave an extra $1 million to the island's directors to "improve their care of the insane."

Nellie had blazed a trail for serious female reporters. She had shown the value of a woman's testimony. Best of all, she had told the public about the conditions of an insane asylum. She helped bring about much-needed reform.

Nellie Bly, Investigative Reporter

These excerpts come from the series of newspaper articles Nellie Bly wrote after she was released from the mental hospital.

"What, excepting torture, would produce insanity quicker than this treatment? Here are women sent to be cured. I would like the expert physicians . . . to take a perfectly sane and healthy woman, shut her up and make her sit from 6 A.M. until 8 P.M. on straight-back benches, do not allow her to talk or move during these hours, give her no reading and let her know nothing of the world, give her bad food and harsh treatment, and see how long it will take to make her insane."

"I lay in bed picturing to myself the horrors in case a fire should break out in the asylum. Every door is locked separately and the windows are heavily barred, so that escape is impossible. In the one building alone there are some 300 women. They are locked, one to ten to a room. It is impossible to get out unless these doors are unlocked. Should the building burn, the nurses would never think of releasing their crazy patients. This I can prove to you later when I tell of their cruel treatment of the poor things entrusted to their care. In case of fire, not a dozen women could escape. All would be left to roast to death."

"'Urena', said [the nurse], 'the doctors say that you are 33 instead of 18,' and the other nurses laughed. After they had gotten all the amusement out of her they wanted and she was crying, they began to tell her to keep quiet. She grew more hysterical every moment until they slapped her face and knocked her head . . . this made the poor creature cry more, and so they choked her. Yes, actually choked her! Then they dragged her out to the closet, and I heard her terrified cries hush into smothered ones."

"Louise Schanz was consigned to the asylum without a chance of making herself understood. Can such carelessness be excused, I wonder, when it is so easy to get an interpreter? Here was a woman taken without her own consent from the free world to an asylum and given no chance to prove her sanity. Confined most probably for life behind asylum bars, without even being told in her language the why and wherefore. Compare this with a criminal, who is given every chance to prove his innocence. Who would not rather be a murderer . . . than be declared insane, without hope of escape? Mrs. Schanz begged in German to know where she was, and pleaded for liberty. Her voice broken by sobs, she was led unheard out to us."

"I left the insane ward with pleasure and regret—pleasure that I was once more able to enjoy the free breath of heaven; regret that I could not have brought with me some of the unfortunate women who lived and suffered with me, and who, I am convinced, are just as sane as I am."

Bly, Nellie, 1887. "Ten Days in a Mad-House."
http://digital.library.upenn.edu/women/bly/madhouse/madhouse.html

Nellie Bly, Investigative Reporter

1. How long was Nellie Bly a patient at the Women's Lunatic Asylum?

a. one week

b. ten days

c. two weeks

d. one month

2. After being a patient at the Women's Lunatic Asylum, Bly believed that

a. all of the women there were sane.

b. all of the women there were insane.

c. the doctors and nurses took good care of the patients.

d. many women were committed too easily.

3. If a patient died at the Women's Lunatic Asylum, it was

a. shocking and rare.

b. a reason to ask the government for more money.

c. viewed as keeping the island's population under control.

d. thoroughly investigated by the police.

4. Nellie Bly felt that the care of the insane should be improved. True or False? Use specific examples to explain your answer.

_____

_____

_____

5. Why did the jury believe Nellie even though the conditions they saw at the Women's Lunatic Asylum were not as bad as she had described?

_____

_____

_____

_____

6. After reading Nellie's news articles, which story did you find more upsetting—Urena's or Louise Schanz's? Why?

_____

_____

_____

_____

Susan B. Anthony, Suffragist

In 1872 Susan B. Anthony was arrested. Her crime? Voting! Anthony had read the Fourteenth Amendment to the U.S. Constitution. It stated, "All persons born or naturalized in the United States . . . are citizens of the United States." The Fifteenth Amendment stated, "The right of citizens of the United States to vote shall not be denied . . on account of race, color, or previous servitude (slavery)." Anthony knew that she had the right to vote. So she went to the polling place, registered, and voted. But at that time women could not vote! They didn't get that right until April 26, 1920. That's when the Nineteenth Amendment was adopted. Unfortunately, Anthony died 14 years before that. But she was an important suffragist. As such, she worked tirelessly for the right of women to vote.

Anthony knew that she would probably be arrested for voting. But she wanted to make the news. Not because she wanted fame, but because she wanted to bring the public's attention to the issue of women voting.

Courtesy of the Library of Congress,
"Susan B. Anthony," LC-DIG-ggbain-30126

When the deputy knocked on her door, he told the gray-haired woman that she was under arrest. But he added that she could just meet him at his office when she was ready. He did not need to escort her. Clearly she was no criminal. Yet Anthony said she would come immediately. So he led her to the streetcar. The conductor asked for her fare. She announced so that all could hear, "I am traveling at the expense of the government. This gentleman is taking me to jail. Ask him for my fare."

Anthony paid bail and was set free. Then she spoke everywhere she could to highlight her cause. At her trial, the judge acted crazy. He was so angry that she had tried to vote that he immediately pronounced her guilty. He would not let Anthony speak. He said that women were not competent to be witnesses in court. He ordered the jury to render a guilty verdict. Then he dismissed them before they could even vote!

The judge fined Anthony $100 plus court costs. Anthony told him that she would never pay it, and she never did. But the judge did not dare to put her in jail. She had promised to appeal to the U.S. Supreme Court. If she did, he feared that she might win. So Anthony went free. She continued her fight for women to vote until the day she died.

Susan B. Anthony, Suffragist

1820	Susan Brownell Anthony born on February 15 in Adams, MA.
1845	The Anthony family moves to Rochester, NY. Their home is a meeting place for anti-slavery activists.
1846	Susan B. Anthony starts teaching at Canajoharie Academy.
1851	Anthony goes to an anti-slavery convention and meets Elizabeth Cady Stanton.
1852	Anthony attends her first women's rights convention.
1854	Anthony circulates petitions for married women's property rights and women's suffrage. She is denied permission to speak at the Capitol and Smithsonian Institution in Washington, D.C. So, speaking and traveling alone, she starts a New York state campaign for women's suffrage (voting rights).
1856	Anthony becomes an agent for the American Anti-Slavery Society.
1857	At a New York State Teachers Convention, Anthony calls for education for women and blacks.
1861	Anthony conducts an anti-slavery campaign from Buffalo to Albany. Her slogan: "No Union with Slaveholders. No Compromise."
1863	Anthony and Stanton co-author *Appeal to the Women of the Republic*.
1868	Anthony begins publication of the newsletter *The Revolution*.
1869	Anthony holds the first Woman Suffrage Convention in Washington D.C.
1872	Anthony votes and is arrested. She keeps lecturing and going to conventions.
1873	At her trial Anthony is fined $100. She refuses to pay but is not jailed.
1898	*The Life and Work of Susan B. Anthony, A Story of the Evolution of the Status of Women* is published. Anthony sets up a press bureau to send articles on woman suffrage to the national and local press.
1905	Anthony meets with President Theodore Roosevelt about submitting a suffrage amendment to Congress.
1906	Anthony attends suffrage hearings in Washington, D.C. On her 86th birthday, she gives her "Failure is Impossible" speech. She dies at her home on March 13.

Susan B. Anthony, Suffragist

1. Susan B. Anthony died in

  a. 1872.

  b. 1906.

  c. 1914.

  d. 1920.

2. A suffragist was a person who worked to

  a. free the slaves.

  b. save the environment.

  c. obtain women's right to vote.

  d. get free health care for all U.S. citizens.

3. Anthony wanted to publicize her arrest for voting because she

  a. hated the U.S. government.

  b. wanted people to discuss the issue of women voting.

  c. hoped to raise money to clean up the environment.

  d. wanted to become infamous.

4. Women's rights was the only cause for which Anthony worked. True or False? Explain.

_____

_____

_____

5. What were Anthony's main goals for women, and how many years passed between her initial interest in women's issues and her death?

_____

_____

_____

_____

6. Would Anthony have been more successful if she had focused solely on women's suffrage? Defend your stance.

_____

_____

_____

_____

Dr. Abel Wolman, Public Health Engineer

Dr. Abel Wolman has saved so many lives that no one can keep count. How? He worked with Linn Enslow to perfect a formula to use chlorine to clean water. Many people feel that this was the most important contribution to public health in the twentieth century.

Dirty drinking water used to spread disease and death. Cholera, yellow fever, and typhoid fever were common. These diseases could be passed from person to person. But they spread the fastest through dirty water. In fact, before 1935, as many Americans died of typhoid fever each year as the number who die in car crashes today.

In 1919 Wolman and Enslow found a way to safely chlorinate water using the least possible amount. But they had to convince the water utilities to act. Most did not want to put a poison into the water. Wolman persisted. He wrote articles. He made speeches. He wouldn't let the matter drop. And once his methods were applied to water supplies nationwide, the death rate from water-borne diseases fell. At the same time the life span of Americans increased.

When Wolman saw the positive impact that clean water had on Americans' health, he wanted people worldwide to have clean water. So he served as an advisor to more than 50 nations and the World Health Organization (WHO). He worked to help them improve water quality.

Today Wolman's methods are still used. If you live in a city, here's how you get your water. First the water is collected in a reservoir. This can be manmade or a lake. When the water is needed, it flows into a building. Chlorine is added there to kill bacteria. Then alum is put into the water. This makes dirt particles clump.

Next the water is stirred with huge mixing paddles. When the paddles stop, the water is still. This lets all of the solids fall to the bottom. The clear water at the top of the tank runs through a gravity sand filter. Then lime is added to reduce the acidity. (Acid would ruin metal pipes.) Often fluoride is put in, too. This chemical strengthens teeth.

The water is left in a reservoir. As it is pulled from the tank, it gets an extra shot of chlorine to sterilize it again. The water moves through pipes by gravity or is pumped into elevated storage tanks. From there, it flows to your faucet.

Dr. Abel Wolman, Public Health Engineer

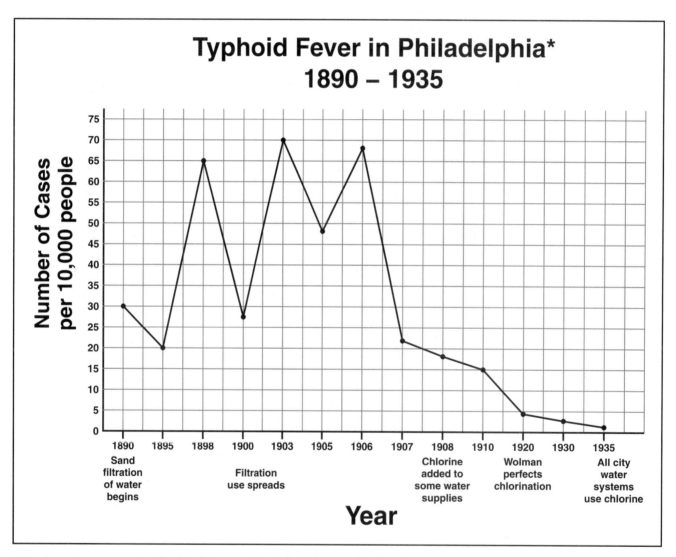

Typhoid Fever in Philadelphia*
1890 – 1935

*During these years Philadelphia was the third-largest city in the United States. It was one of the first places to use sand filtration and chlorination to treat its drinking water.

Statistics from Davis, Mackenzie L. and David A Cornwell.
Introduction to Environmental Engineering. Boston: PWS Publisher, 1985.

Dr. Abel Wolman, Public Health Engineer

1. Alum is added to drinking water to

  a. reduce the acid level.

  b. sterilize the water.

  c. make dirt pieces in water clump together.

  d. strengthen people's teeth.

2. About how long did it take for all Philadelphia water utilities to use Wolman's chlorination method?

  a. 2 years

  b. 4 years

  c. 11 years

  d. 16 years

3. Why does Abel Wolman get more credit for creating pure drinking water than Linn Enslow?

  a. because Enslow had nothing to do with inventing sand filtration

  b. because Wolman kept after the water utilities to use chlorination and later worked with WHO to improve water quality worldwide

  c. because Enslow died while the men were perfecting the chlorination formula

  d. because Wolman denied that Enslow had ever helped him with the chlorination formula

4. Sand filtration of drinking water was first used in Philadelphia in 1880 and is still used today. True or False? Explain.

_____

_____

_____

5. Look at the line graph. In what year was chlorine first added to the Philadelphia water supply, and was it soon obvious that it helped to curb typhoid fever?

_____

_____

_____

_____

6. Were the people in charge of the water utilities throughout America wrong not to adopt Wolman's chlorination method immediately? Defend your stance.

_____

_____

_____

_____

The Heroism of Chiune Sugihara

Chiune Sugihara was a Japanese diplomat. He lived with his family in an embassy in Lithuania. In late July 1940 hundreds of Jews escaped from Poland. They stood outside his gate and begged Sugihara to write them visas to Japan. The Nazis were fast approaching. But the people could not leave the nation without a visa. They had to escape, yet they were trapped.

These Jews needed to stay ahead of the Nazis. The Nazis wanted to kill all of them. They did this by sending the Jews to concentration camps. There the people had to do hard work. They were barely fed. If they got ill, they received no medical care. Some people never had a chance. As soon as they stepped off the train, they were sent to a gas chamber to die. Millions perished and whole families were wiped out. One of the worst of death camps was Auschwitz.

Three times Sugihara asked the Japanese government for permission to write these visas. Every time he was refused. He gathered his wife, two small sons, and sister. They talked about what to do. With his family's support, Sugihara made a dangerous decision. He would write a visa for every Jew. If caught, he and his family would face jail or death.

Each visa had to be handwritten. Sugihara wrote from dawn to dark. His arm cramped, and his shoulder ached, but he kept writing. He would not let his wife or sister write a single one. He wanted to take full responsibility.

The Russian army entered the nation. They told the Sugiharas to leave. As punishment for his deeds, the whole family was imprisoned for 18 months in Romania. When they were released, they went to Japan. He was fired and disgraced for writing the visas. He could never work for the Japanese government again.

This brave man had saved thousands of Jews from the Nazis' death camps. His courage earned him the Righteous Among the Nations Award. It was given at the Yad Vashem Holocaust memorial in Israel in 1985. Today he has a monument in his birthplace of Yaotsu, Japan. It is called the Hill of Humanity.

The Heroism of Chiune Sugihara

August 26, 1946

Dear Mr. Sugihara,

I hope that you are alive and this letter finds its way to you. I do not know if you can read what I have written. I know that Japanese people do not use letters as my language does. Maybe you can find someone to read this to you.

I want to thank you for giving me and my two children visas to leave Lithuania. I will spare you the details of all our adventures after we left you. We finally found asylum * in Switzerland and lived there for the remainder of the war. All of our family and friends who did not escape the Warsaw ghetto died in the death camps. My beloved husband Matthew, who was taken before we fled to Lithuania, died in Auschwitz.

I can't express the depth of my gratitude for what you did to save me and my daughter and son. Without the visas you prepared for us, we would surely have perished. Now we are struggling to rebuild our lives in Poland, but at least we have each other. That is so much more than many other Jews have.

I have worried about you and prayed for you and your family all these years. I know that you risked your children's lives to save mine. You are so courageous. I hope you and your family survived the war. Please know that you will always have a place in my heart, and I will never forget you.

Gratefully yours,

Marta Goldstein and family

*safety

The Heroism of Chiune Sugihara

1. Chiune Sugihara was originally from

    a. Poland.   c. Lithuania.

    b. Romania.   d. Japan.

2. By writing visas for the Jews, Sugihara was disobeying

    a. the Japanese government.   c. international laws.

    b. the Lithuanian government.   d. the Romanian government.

3. Most of the Jews for whom Sugihara wrote visas

    a. traveled to Japan.   c. sold the visas on the black market.

    b. used the visas to leave Lithuania.   d. used the visas to get out of
                                           concentration camps.

4. Sugihara's family members were not punished because Sugihara wrote the visas for the Jews. True or False. Explain.

_____

_____

_____

5. Why did Marta Goldstein write to Sugihara? What happened to her husband, her son, and her daughter? Why does she write that she has more than many other Jews?

_____

_____

_____

_____

_____

6. Did the Japanese government do the right thing by firing Sugihara? Defend your stance.

_____

_____

_____

_____

_____

Nelson Mandela: A Man of Courage

Nelson Mandela spent over 27 years in jail. Most of these years he spent on a small limestone rock island. He worked on a labor crew. They pounded boulders into gravel. It was hard work. But for Mandela, the hardest part of his imprisonment was the lack of contact with his family.

Mandela could not get mail. When he was allowed a rare visit, it took place in a crude wooden shack at the end of the island. The warden listened to every word. Mandela's family members did not have enough money to take time off from work or pay the travel fees. And since the prison was more than 900 miles away from their home, he rarely saw them.

What was this man's crime? Mandela had spoken out against apartheid. Apartheid was the forced separation of whites and blacks. He was a black South African. At that time, South Africa was ruled by a white minority government. Millions of black Africans could not vote. They could not go to the same schools or live in the same neighborhoods as whites. Native South Africans could only go to certain beaches and hospitals. They could only join certain sports teams and sit in certain seats on buses or trains.

The entire time that Mandela was in jail he never lost his dignity or courage. He knew that all people were equal and should have the same rights. At that time, South African leaders "banned" people who wanted to make changes. A banned person could not be in a group of more than three people, even inside his or her own home. For the whole time Mandela was imprisoned, he was banned. He'd been banned even before he was sent there. It made it hard for him to practice law. He did not stop going to his office. But he had to go at night. Despite being banned and jailed, his fellow citizens saw him as the leader of the anti-apartheid movement.

World leaders put pressure on the South African government. They demanded Mandela's release. At last the nation's rulers knew that they would have to change. The cry for freedom and equality could not be silenced. In February 1990, Mandela was set free. Around the world people of all colors cheered for him. He immediately tried to gain political power for the nation's blacks in a peaceful way. So in 1993 he won the Nobel Peace Prize. The next year he was elected the president of South Africa. In December 1996 Mandela signed into law the new South African constitution. It guaranteed freedom of speech and all people's rights.

Nelson Mandela: A Man of Courage

Here are excerpts from Nelson Mandela's Nobel Peace Prize speech given in 1993:

"We stand here today as nothing more than a representative of the millions of our people who dared to rise up against a social system whose very essence is war, violence, racism, oppression, repression and the impoverishment of an entire people."

"I am also here today as a representative of the millions of people across the globe, the anti-apartheid movement, the governments and organisations that joined with us, not to fight against South Africa as a country or any of its peoples, but to oppose an inhuman system and sue for a speedy end to the apartheid crime against humanity."

"These countless human beings, both inside and outside our country, had the nobility of spirit to stand in the path of tyranny and injustice, without seeking selfish gain. They recognised that an injury to one is an injury to all and therefore acted together in defense of justice and a common human decency."

© The Nobel Foundation 1993. Used with permission.
Mandela, Nelson. "Nobel Peace Prize Acceptance Address."
http://nobelprize.virtual.museum/nobel_prizes/peace/laureates/1993/mandela-lecture.html

Nelson Mandela: A Man of Courage

1. As a banned person, Nelson Mandela could not
   - a. write letters.
   - b. get together with a big group of people.
   - c. go anywhere in a car.
   - d. hold a job.

2. Mandela's story is most similar to
   - a. Susan B. Anthony's struggle to get women the right to vote.
   - b. Harriet Tubman's repeated trips to help slaves to freedom on the Underground Railroad.
   - c. Martin Luther King, Jr.'s struggle to get civil rights for African Americans in the United States.
   - d. George Washington's battle to free Americans from Great Britain's control.

3. Apartheid is a kind of
   - a. damage to the environment.
   - b. education.
   - c. financial system.
   - d. racism.

4. Mandela was imprisoned because he had committed a crime against a South African leader. True or False? Explain your answer.

   _____

   _____

   _____

5. In his Nobel Peace Prize speech, to whom does Mandela give credit for ending apartheid in South Africa? Why?

   _____

   _____

   _____

   _____

   _____

6. After Mandela became president of South Africa, should he have imprisoned the former leaders who had enforced apartheid? Defend your stance.

   _____

   _____

   _____

   _____

   _____

Poisonous Animals

Did you know that bright-colored butterflies are toxic? Not to us, but to predators. The bright colors warn bats, mice, birds, and lizards not to eat the butterfly. Not only will it taste bad, it will make the predator ill. The monarch is one such butterfly. However, not all colorful butterflies have poison; some just copy the look of the toxic ones in order to fool predators.

Poison dart frogs have skin glands that make a bad-tasting toxin. It protects them from predators. This poison will kill an animal if it grabs the frog. People can get sick just from touching the frog's skin! (The poison dart frogs that people keep as pets don't have this strong poison because it comes from eating bugs they can only get in the wild.) Toads, another amphibian, also use poison to scare away predators. Every adult toad has some poison, but the world's largest, the African cane toad, has the most. These toads can reach 5.5 pounds! Big lumps behind the eyes fill with a poison that looks like white glue. When a predator grabs the toad, it tastes this poison and quickly spits it out.

Although butterflies, poison dart frogs, and toads may have poison, they are not venomous animals. Venomous animals put poison into their victims with stingers, fangs, or tentacles. Not all are deadly. Stingrays, which are related to sharks, are venomous. Born alive, they look like tiny adults. They have a stinger near their tails. But they are rarely aggressive. Most people who get stung do so by accidentally stepping on a stingray. Its poison will make a person throw up. However, if the sting occurs near the heart, it can be fatal.

Scorpions live in the desert. They don't often come across animals, so when they do, they must make a kill. They sting their prey with a toxin. It liquefies the victim's internal tissues. Then the scorpion sucks out the animal's innards. Yuck!

Tarantulas have hairy bodies and legs. These hairs have barbs that stick into skin. If this happens, a doctor must remove them with a special tool. The tarantula's poison is identical to a bee's. Yet its sting feels much worse. Even so, Mexicans use tarantula silk, collected from the spinnerets, to make shirts and hats.

The wandering spider lives further south in the Amazon rain forest. As the deadliest spider on Earth, its venom is 18 times stronger than a black widow spider's! Nobody wants to get near one. It is so aggressive that it will jump onto a person or an animal.

Striped sea snakes are the only reptiles that spend their entire lives in water. They have such strong venom that their bite kills a human within seven minutes! A bite from a rattlesnake or a cobra is also fatal. But with their bites, there is time to get an antidote.

Poisonous Animals

Want to know more about venomous animals?
Visit the new Toxic Terrors Exhibit
at the Learning Pavilion
City of Cedarhurst Zoo
June 20—October 5

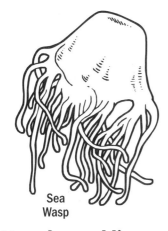

Sea
Wasp

**Meet the world's most
venomous animal!**

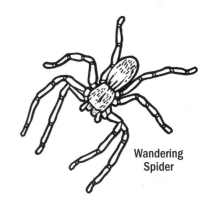

Wandering
Spider

**Watch the deadly wandering
spider make its web!**

Striped
Sea Snake

**See the world's most
poisonous snake!**

Monarch
Butterfly

**Did you know that a monarch
butterfly is toxic?**

You'll be surprised by some of the animals you see!

Poisonous Animals

1. Which animal is venomous?

    a. poison dart frog   c. Monarch butterfly

    b. scorpion   d. African cane toad

2. Which of these is a reptile?

    a. scorpion   c. poison dart frog

    b. stingray   d. striped sea snake

3. If an animal is aggressive, it

    a. attacks other animals.   c. has camouflage coloring.

    b. hides from other animals.   d. is always venomous.

4. The most venomous animal in the world is the striped sea snake. True or False? Explain.

_____

_____

_____

5. Describe what the Cedarhurst Zoo must do in order to keep visitors safe in the Toxic Terrors exhibit.

_____

_____

_____

_____

_____

6. Which one of the poisonous animals mentioned in the article is the most frightening? Why?

_____

_____

_____

_____

_____

The Story of *Exodus 1947*

The *President Warfield* was built in 1928 to carry passengers for the Baltimore Steam Packet Company. In World War II, many ships were taken over by the U.S. government. They were needed to move troops. The *President Warfield* was no exception. It carried soldiers from the shores of England to the beaches of Normandy for the famous D-Day battle in June 1944.

In 1946, a Jewish group named Haganah bought the ship. This group renamed it *Exodus 1947*. In March 1947 it set sail with 4,515 immigrants. They were Jews. Most of them had lived through the Holocaust. During the Holocaust, Nazi Germany tried to kill every Jew. They put them into concentration camps. There they worked the people to death or killed them in gas chambers.

Many Jews that survived until the end of World War II had lost all they owned. They had no homes to which to return. So they planned to settle Israel. This new nation had been part of Palestine. But the peace treaty that ended World War II made it a homeland for the Jews. People hoped that this would prevent another Holocaust.

Great Britain did not want the Jews to go to Israel. It tried to enforce a League of Nations 1923 decree. This rule let Jews live in Palestine only if they did not impose on the rights of the non-Jews already there. Great Britain felt that the creation of Israel imposed on the rights of the Palestinians. And the new nation's creation would make the Middle East unstable. So a British ship rammed the *Exodus 1947*. Three people aboard were killed. Thirty were hurt. The ship could not go on. The British towed it to Haifa, a port in what is now Israel.

They sent the war-weary refugees to camps in Hamburg, Germany! The British now controlled these camps. The people were not mistreated. But the walls had barbed wire. Movement in and out of the camps was limited. They felt like prisoners.

The nation of Israel was established on May 14, 1948. By that August, most of the people had moved there on their own. In 1951, plans were made to turn *Exodus 1947* into a floating museum. But the next summer, it caught fire. The ship was destroyed. It lies submerged near Haifa, Israel.

The Story of *Exodus 1947*

This is a note written by an anonymous Jew who was aboard *Exodus 1947*:

British soldiers and officers!

You are waging a battle against peaceful innocent people, which only crime consists in that they want a home just like hundreds of people and millions of peoples in the world!

We have been dragged away with brutality from the shores of Palestine, and for about two month already we are being led on the sea locked in behind barbed wire, just if we were dangerous criminals. Now you want get us off with force in Hamburg [Germany] back to our enemies, back to the murder people, which wanted annihilate the world, and bestially* destroyed our parents and children and exterminated more than a third of our people. You are sending us back to pains, sufferings, and downfall!!

British soldiers and officers!

To day you are compelled to do the same thing the Germans did before, against whom you fought so heroically!

Put no shame on your glorious tradition of fight against fascism.** Put yourselves on the side of the victims of Hitlerism! Allow us to go home so that once and for all we will be able to live as free people!

No force in the world can destroy our will to live!

Until our last breath we will always aim for Palestine. Our spirit is always strong and invincible!!!

We are the rightful!

Ours is the future!

*cruelly, savagely

**extreme nationalistic beliefs and strict obedience to the leader of the state; Nazism was a form of fascism

Exodus 1947 Home page. **www.exodus1947.org**

The Story of *Exodus 1947*

1. The ship named *Exodus 1947* was originally built to carry

    a. refugees to Israel.

    b. troops in World War II.

    c. passengers in the United States.

    d. refugees to Germany.

2. Today's Israel was once part of the nation of

    a. Palestine.

    b. Great Britain.

    c. Germany.

    d. Haifa.

3. The nation of Israel was established by

    a. the League of Nations.

    b. Haganah.

    c. Great Britain.

    d. the peace treaty that ended World War II.

4. It was wrong to house the Jewish refugees in German camps. True or False? Explain.

_____

_____

_____

5. How is the note's author trying to make the British soldiers and officers feel? Use quotes from the note to support your response.

_____

_____

_____

6. Should the British have interfered with the *Exodus 1947*? Defend your stance.

_____

_____

_____

_____

_____

Roanoke Island's Lost Colony

Did you know that the first English colony in America vanished, and no one knows what happened to it? A group of families went to live on Roanoke Island, which lies off the coast of what is now North Carolina. They arrived in July 1587. John White was their governor. Soon a friendly male Native American named Manteo joined their group.

Not long after the settlers arrived, they found one of their men dead. Fear swept over the colonists. They assumed the Roanoke tribe that lived on the mainland had killed him. The English attacked their village. Later they found out that the Roanokes had fled, and the people in the village had been a friendly Croatoan tribe gathering the things the others had left behind! Manteo tried to patch up things with the Croatoans, but no one knows if the Native Americans forgave the settlers.

One month later, White decided to go back for supplies. The settlers promised that if they had to leave the island they would carve their destination on a tree. If they were in trouble, they would carve a cross above it. When White left for England, he had no idea that he would never see any of them again.

White arrived in England to find war raging between his country and Spain. All ships were needed for battle, so he could not return. For over two years, the Roanoke settlers had no contact with England. White sailed back in 1590. When he arrived, the homes were in ruins. Large trees formed a fence around the village, making what looked like a crude fort. White found a tree with the letters CRO. A fence post had "Croatoan" carved on it. Neither one had a cross. White thought that the settlers had gone to Croatoan Island. He and his crew planned to sail there. But a hurricane blew them so far out to sea that they had to return to England. White never raised the funds needed to return.

What happened to the Roanoke colony, which had been the home of 113 people? Today scientists know that a bad drought (lack of rain) occurred in the area. The people may have died of starvation due to the drought. Maybe they merged with a Native American tribe. Native Americans may have killed the settlers. Or perhaps they set sail for home and were shipwrecked.

In 1588, the Spanish sent explorers to the area. They saw no white people or dead bodies. In 1607, a Native American chief told settlers in Virginia that he had killed the people at Roanoke. But in 1709, John Lawson spent time with the Croatoans. He said that many of natives looked white. Some even had blue eyes, which was unknown among Native Americans.

In the 1800s, the Croatoans changed their tribe name to Lumbee. The Lumbees, the largest tribe east of the Mississippi River, live in North Carolina. They say that they are the descendants of the lost colonists and Native Americans.

Roanoke Island's Lost Colony

Theory	Pros	Cons
The colonists set sail for England and were shipwrecked.	They wanted to go home and might have been able to build a ship.	They had just one small boat for 113 people. The colonists were far too busy staying alive (building homes, growing food) to have the time to build a ship.
The colonists were all killed during a surprise Native American attack.	If the attack happened soon after White left, three years later there would be little evidence. The carved "Croatoan" might have been their way of identifying their killers.	The colonists were heavily armed. It seems unlikely that someone had time to carve words during an attack.
The colonists were killed by a strong hurricane. The few survivors merged with the Croatoan tribe.	If the people were swept out to sea in a storm surge, it would explain their disappearance. Afterwards, a couple of survivors may have carved "Croatoan."	The damage to the buildings and fence did not look like it had been done by a hurricane. Of course, White was unfamiliar with such storms since he came from England, which doesn't have them.
The colonists merged with the Croatoan tribe, probably because they were starving due to a drought.	There is evidence of a bad drought at that time. Croatoans (now Lumbees) have blue eyes, "white" facial features, and lighter skin color. Their language includes words from 16th century English. The Lumbees insist that this is their oral history tradition.	Historians say these things are probably the result of later contact with Europeans.
The colonists split into two groups. One went to Croatoan Island. The other went to the Chesapeake Bay area. The Lumbees absorbed the first group. Chief Powhatan killed the second.	Powhatan told John Smith of Jamestown, Virginia this information. Powhatan said that he didn't want the two groups of whites to team up against his tribe.	John Smith may not be a reliable witness. Much of his writing about his New World adventures are considered fantasies by modern scholars.

Roanoke Island's Lost Colony

1. The Croatoan tribe was renamed in
   a. 1590.
   b. 1607.
   c. 1709.
   d. the 1800s.

2. When he returned from England, John White thought that the settlers had moved to Croatoan Island because
   a. there was a crude fort around the village.
   b. a settler had left a note stating that that's where they were going.
   c. a fence post had "Croatoan" carved on it.
   d. their homes had been ruined.

3. What convinced John Lawson that the Roanoke settlers had merged with a Native American tribe?
   a. some of the Native Americans had blue eyes and light skin
   b. one of the colonists had carved a tribe name on a post
   c. he talked to the last remaining settlers
   d. he read about it in a settler's diary that the Native Americans gave him

4. The colonists started out on the wrong foot with the area Native American tribes. True or False? Explain.

   _____

   _____

   _____

5. List the reasons why historians question the idea that all of the settlers were killed in a surprise Native American attack.

   _____

   _____

   _____

   _____

   _____

6. Which theory do you believe explains what happened to the Roanoke settlers? Defend your stance.

   _____

   _____

   _____

   _____

   _____

Trash: It's Got to Go Somewhere

As long as there have been people, there's been trash. In the United States, beginning in colonial days, people in rural areas just threw their trash in one spot on their property. The plant and animal materials rotted. The rest just piled up. Getting rid of trash has always been a bigger problem in cities. There just wasn't space available for junk to pile up. So towns had bands of roaming wild dogs and pigs. They ate a lot of the refuse. But the things that they couldn't eat were still left behind.

Starting in the 1800s, most U.S. cities had garbage carts. Horses drew these carts. The driver announced his arrival with a trumpet. When the people heard the trumpet, they brought out their trash and loaded it onto the cart themselves. (This practice lasted until about 1935.)

The trash was taken to the city's incinerator. However, not everything could go into this furnace. So women sorted through the garbage on the carts. They pulled out metal, glass, and any other things that wouldn't readily burn. The metal and glass were bundled and put up for sale. If no one bought this scrap, the items would be buried.

Today each American creates about four pounds of trash daily. Trucks come to people's homes to gather the trash. Where does it all go? About 20 percent is burned to make steam or electricity. About 45 percent is buried in a landfill or dumped far out in the ocean. After garbage trucks dump waste at a landfill, bulldozers compress the material. It's covered with soil daily. This prevents the trash from blowing around and odors from escaping. But it means that little oxygen or water reaches the waste, making it decay slowly. As the materials rot, they send methane gas fumes through pipes. These vents are placed in the landfill for this purpose. Rainwater also seeps into the landfill. Sanitary landfills have heavy plastic or clay liners to contain the water. A drainage system sends the trapped water to a sewage treatment plant.

Only about 35 percent of all solid waste is recycled. That percentage should be higher. Much of the paper, plastic, glass, and metal that can be recycled is not. That's because people throw it in the trash can instead of the recycle bin. A recent study showed that people are most apt to recycle if they have curbside pickup instead of having to take the materials to a center. People are also most likely to recycle if landfill space is in short supply.

Trash: It's Got to Go Somewhere

Total Trash Generated in 2003 in U.S. (before recycling)

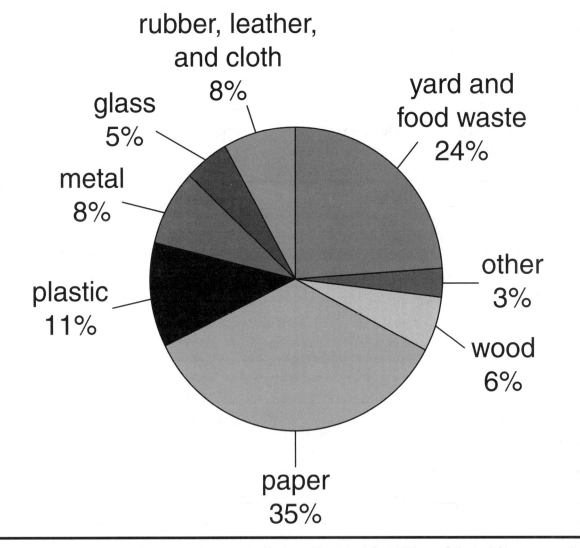

rubber, leather, and cloth 8%

glass 5%

metal 8%

plastic 11%

yard and food waste 24%

other 3%

wood 6%

paper 35%

U.S. Environmental Protection Agency. Municipal Solid Waste Generation, Recycling, and Disposal in the United States, 2003.

Trash: It's Got to Go Somewhere

1. Landfills have liners in order to keep

   a. polluted water from getting
      into the groundwater.

   b. solid waste from rotting.

   c. the trash from blowing around.

   d. odors from escaping.

2. Most of the United States' solid waste is

   a. recycled.

   b. buried in a landfill or dumped in the ocean.

   c. burned to make steam or electricity.

   d. sent into outer space.

3. An incinerator is a type of

   a. landfill.

   b. recycling center.

   c. trash pick up.

   d. furnace.

4. People are most likely to recycle when they must take materials to a recycling center. True or
   False? Explain.

   _____

   _____

   _____

5. Name three items included in the "other" category of the pie graph. (Hint: Think about the
   things in your home.)

   _____

   _____

   _____

   _____

   _____

6. Should recycling be required and a big fine charged to anyone who fails to recycle? Defend your
   stance.

   _____

   _____

   _____

   _____

   _____

Alien Species Wreak Havoc

An alien species is not one from outer space. It is any animal brought into an environment where it had never been before. Bringing an alien species into an environment is often bad news. In 1955, the people in South America imported African bees. They thought they would breed with the native bees to create more productive honeybees. But their plan backfired. When the bees bred with the native bees, the gentle bees became aggressive. These new, dangerous bees are killer bees. They will chase a person and cover his or her body in stings. Many people die from receiving so many stings. These bees focus their attack on carbon dioxide—which is what we breathe out! They can track a person for many yards. Killer bees nest in the ground. When a person passes by, they send out huge swarms of guard bees. They have five times the number of guard bees that normal honeybees have.

More than 30 years ago, Asian carp were imported to farms in Arkansas. They were supposed to clean algae from ponds. Flooding swept them into the Illinois River. These fish are not very tasty. And now they are destroying the food source of fish that are good to eat. People don't want Asian carp to spread into the Great Lakes. So there are now underwater electrical gates to prevent them from entering Lake Michigan.

The coqui frog is native to Puerto Rico. The environment there is similar to the one in Hawaii. But there had never been coqui frogs in Hawaii. That changed when plants from Puerto Rico were brought to Hawaii. The tiny frogs hitched rides on these plants. They got into the environment and are causing havoc. Why? Hawaii has no native frogs. Native predators did not know what these animals were. They would not eat them. Now every three feet there's a coqui frog. On every acre there are an estimated 12,000! They are eating insects faster than the bugs can reproduce. As a result, Hawaii's unique insects are endangered.

Brown tree snakes have caused big trouble in Guam. The snakes slithered onto ships docked in their native Australia and Papua New Guinea. Then they slithered off in Guam. Without natural predators, nothing kept their numbers in check. Their numbers grew out of control, and they have wiped out many native bird, small mammal, and lizard species.

Alien Species Wreak Havoc

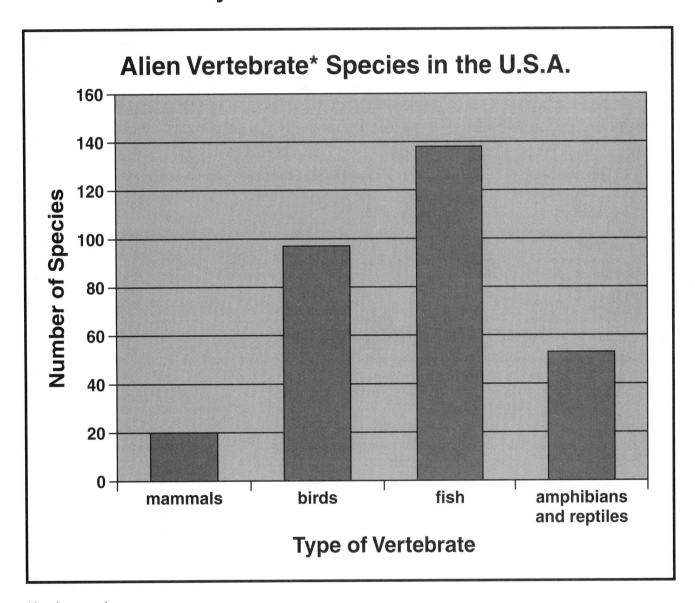

*having a spine

Pimentel, David, et al. "Environmental and Economic Costs Associated with Non-Indigenous Species in the United States." **www.news.cornell.edu/releases/Jan99/species_costs.html**

Alien Species Wreak Havoc

1. What alien species is causing trouble for Guam?

    a. Asian carp

    b. African bees

    c. brown tree snakes

    d. coqui frogs

2. Why do people die from killer bees?

    a. The people receive multiple stings.

    b. The bees follow the carbon dioxide right into a person's lungs.

    c. Guard bees chase the people until they have heart attacks.

    d. The bees cause blood vessels to burst in the people's brains.

3. From this article, you can tell that alien species may be dangerous to an area's

    a. predators

    b. prey

    c. people

    d. all of the above

4. Asian carp were imported to clean up the Illinois River. True or False? Explain.

_____

_____

_____

5. Name the types of alien vertebrates that have the highest and the lowest numbers of species in the U.S.A.

_____

_____

_____

_____

6. Should alien species be killed using whatever means is necessary to get rid of them? Defend your stance.

_____

_____

_____

_____

U.S. Anti-Slave Trade Actions

Did you know that in the early 1800s the U.S. Navy tried to stop slaves from entering the nation? By the late 1700s, the people in America's northern states realized that slavery was wrong. They began to lobby Congress for laws to end this inhumane practice. But Congress was slow to act. This is because there were about the same number of senators from the North and the South. The South's whole economy rested on free labor. The South had many large plantations. To maintain these huge farms took a great deal of manual labor. The people in the South refused to give up slavery.

Still in 1794, Congress made it illegal to outfit slave ships in U.S. ports. Six years later it became illegal for a U.S. citizen to transport slaves for sale from one nation to another.   In 1807, Congress outlawed the trading of slaves between Africa, and the United States. This meant that no new slaves could enter the country. All of these laws tried to stop more people from being enslaved. But they did nothing to help the current slaves or their offspring.

To make matters worse, the rules weren't strictly enforced. Finally, in 1815, the U.S. Navy began to enforce the anti-slave trade laws. It had ships patrol the western coast of Africa. Sailors did not like serving on these ships. They called it hardship duty. Since the climate was hot and humid, they suffered from tropical diseases. Many of the men were sickened by the cruelty they witnessed. And when they captured a ship, they had to nurse the captives back to health. This was often a difficult task.

To motivate men to work on these ships, the United States offered prize money for each captured vessel and $25 for every slave rescued. This money was given to the naval ship's captain. He divided it among the crew based on rank.

When a ship was found to be carrying slaves, it was seized. Then it was sold at auction. Its captain and officers went before the U.S. Federal Court, but the slave ship's crew was set free with the captives. All were put ashore at Monrovia, Liberia.

Slavers continued to avoid or outrun the U.S. ships. Some even dumped their "cargo" into the sea. This way, when the ship was boarded, it was empty and could not be seized. This meant that every captive on the ship was drowned! Yet the captains only faced jail if caught. So in 1820, Congress made transporting slaves by sea an act of piracy. It was punishable by the death penalty.

U.S. Anti-Slave Trade Actions

BY
HEWLETT & BRIGHT
SALE OF
VALUABLE
SLAVES
(on account of departure)

The Owner of the following named and valuable Slaves, being on the eve of departure for Europe, will cause the same to be offered for sale, at the NEW EXCHANGE, corner of St. Louis and Chartres streets, on Saturday, May 16, at Twelve O'Clock.

1.   SARAH, aged 45 years, a good cook and accustomed to housework in general, is an excellent and faithful nurse for sick persons, and in every respect a first rate character.

2.   DENNIS, her son, aged 24 years, a first rate cook and steward for a vessel having been in that capacity for many years on board one of the Mobile packets; is strictly honest, temperate, and a first rate subject.

3.   CHLOE, aged 36 years, she is without exception, one of the most competent servants in the country, a first rate washer and ironer, does up lace, a good cook, and for a bachelor who wishes a house-keeper she would be invaluable; she is also a good ladies' maid, having traveled to the North in that capacity.

4.   FANNY, her daughter, aged 16 years, speaks French and English, is a superior hair-dresser, a good seamstress and ladies' maid, is smart, intelligent, and a first rate character.

5.   DANDRIDGE, aged 26 years, a first rate dining-room servant, a good painter and rough carpenter, and has but few equals for honesty and sobriety.

6.   NANCY, his wife, aged about 24 years, a confidential house servant, a good seamstress, a good cook, washer and ironer, etc.

7.   MARY ANN, their child, aged 7 years, speaks French and English, is smart, active, and intelligent.

8.   FANNY, aged 22 years, is a first rate washer and ironer, good cook and house servant, and has an excellent character.

9.   EMMA, an orphan, aged 10 or 11 years, speaks French and English, has been in the country 7 years, has been accustomed to waiting on table, sewing, etc., is intelligent and active.

10.   FRANK, aged about 32 years, speaks French and English, is a first rate coachman, understands perfectly well the management of horses and is, in every respect, a first rate character, with the exception that he will occasionally drink, though not an habitual drunkard.

All the above named Slaves are acclimated and excellent subjects; they were purchased by their present vendor many years ago, and will, therefore, be severally warranted against all vices and maladies prescribed by law, save and except FRANK, who is fully guaranteed in every other respect but the one above mentioned.

TERMS:—One-half Cash, and the other half in notes at Six months, drawn and endorsed to the satisfaction of the Vendor, with special mortgage on the Slaves until final payment. The Acts of Sale to be passed before WILLIAM BOSWELL, Notary Public, at the expense of the Purchaser.

New-Orleans, May 13, 1835

U.S. Anti-Slave Trade Actions

1. The anti-slave laws passed by Congress helped

    a. people who were already American slaves.

    b. current American slaves' children.

    c. to end slavery worldwide.

    d. to stop more people from becoming American slaves.

2. The crew of a slave ship

    a. had to face trial in U.S. Federal Court.

    b. was put ashore with the captives.

    c. was executed immediately.

    d. went to jail without a trial.

3. Why did slave ship captains sometimes drown their captives?

    a. No one would buy the slaves.

    b. The slaves weren't worth much money.

    c. The slaves were evidence that would result in the ship being seized.

    d. The captain was afraid that that slaves would spread disease.

4. Most U.S. sailors liked to work on the anti-slave ships. True or False? Explain.

    _____

    _____

    _____

5. What is the date on the slave auction poster? How could this auction be taking place when anti-slave trade laws started to be enforced in 1815?

    _____

    _____

    _____

    _____

    _____

6. What was the worst part of slavery? Defend your stance using information from the slave auction poster.

    _____

    _____

    _____

    _____

The U.S. Mint

Did you know that by law the word "liberty" must appear on every U.S. coin? All U.S. coins are minted at one of four locations: Philadelphia, San Francisco, Denver, or West Point. Paper money is printed at the Bureau of Engraving in Washington, D.C., or Fort Worth, Texas.

The coin-making process begins with huge coils of nickel or copper. These coils are 13 inches wide and 1,500 feet long. That's the length of five football fields! Each coil weighs more than four tons. The metal coil unrolls into a press that's like a gigantic cookie cutter. It stamps out two tons of blanks per hour. (The leftover scraps around the edges get recycled.) The blanks are heated in an annealing furnace, then washed, dried, and "upset." Upset is the name of the milling process that smoothes the edges.

The coin presses contain steel dies. Using tons of pressure, the front and back dies strike the coins simultaneously. Coins are struck at a rate of 780 coins per minute. The more valuable the coin, the more pressure is needed to strike it. Pennies need 30 tons of pressure, dimes 46 tons, and quarters 60 tons. Why? Dimes and quarters are clad coins since they have copper centers and an outer layer of nickel. As clad coins are minted, their edges are reeded. Each coin has a mintmark next to the date. The letter tells where the coin was struck. Pennies without a mintmark were made in Philadelphia.

Next, a machine counts the coins. Then they are put into bags and weighed as a double check on the value. They wait in a vault for shipment to a Federal Reserve Bank. After arriving at the Federal Reserve Bank, they wait in its vault. Local banks send their old, worn out coins to a Federal Reserve Bank. Armored trucks bring them back shiny new coins. The coins get put into circulation as the banks distribute them to people. Circulating coins usually wear out after 30 years.

The Philadelphia Mint was the first one in the United States. In 1792, it struck coins by hand using screw presses. It took them three years to make one million coins. Today this mint can produce one million coins in 30 minutes! The Philadelphia Mint makes 18 million pennies and 10 million quarters a day. Each year it mints six billion pennies. That's almost half of all pennies made annually.

The Philadelphia mint designs and strikes all national award medals. The Congressional Gold Medal of Honor is worth about $5,000–$6,000. It is given to people—not necessarily U.S. citizens—for their service to others. Rosa Parks, an African American civil rights leader, received this medal. Other recipients include Mother Teresa and Pope John Paul. Sometimes bronze duplicates are made for collectors to buy.

The U.S. Mint

In The News This Week

The United States Mint in Denver celebrated "100 Years of Change" on February 1, 2006. On February 1, 1906, the Denver Mint's current building opened and struck its first coins on three coining presses.

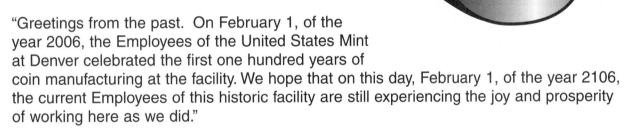

In honor of the 100th anniversary, the Acting Director of the United States Mint and the Plant Manager at the Denver facility prepared a time capsule. It holds a set of 2006 uncirculated coins minted in Denver and a scroll signed by every employee who currently works there. The scroll reads:

"Greetings from the past. On February 1, of the year 2006, the Employees of the United States Mint at Denver celebrated the first one hundred years of coin manufacturing at the facility. We hope that on this day, February 1, of the year 2106, the current Employees of this historic facility are still experiencing the joy and prosperity of working here as we did."

The time capsule also holds a Mayoral Proclamation listing some statistics about the U.S. Mint at Denver. It

- holds a world record for making more than 15 billion circulating coins in one year
- is one of the places in Denver that tourists are most apt to visit
- has an outstanding safety record

On February 1, 2106, workers at the Denver plant will take the capsule from its stone block inside the building and open it.

U.S. Mint. "Spring 2006 Edition of Making Cents."

http://www.usmint.gov/kids/index.cfm?fileContents=coinNews/makingCents/2006/q2.cfm

The U.S. Mint

1. All U.S. paper money is made at the

   a. Federal Reserve Bank.   c. U.S. Mint in Philadelphia.

   b. Bureau of Engraving.   d. U.S. Mint in Washington, D.C.

2. Reeded edges are

   a. used on the least valuable coins.   c. ridged.

   b. silver.   d. smooth.

3. Which coin takes the most pressure to strike?

   a. a penny   c. a dime

   b. a nickel   d. a quarter

4. When the workers open the time capsule in 2106, the U.S. Mint in Denver will be 200 years old. True or False? Explain your answer.

_____

_____

_____

5. For what does the U.S. Mint at Denver hold a world record?

_____

_____

_____

_____

6. Should the Congressional Gold Medal of Honor be given only to U.S. citizens? Defend your stance.

_____

_____

_____

_____

Fit for a King:
The Great Pyramid at Giza

The Egyptians turned their dead royalty into mummies. They thought that for the soul to live forever, the body must be preserved. So they dried and embalmed the dead. Then they wrapped them in linen. From about 2700 to 1700 B.C.E., the bodies of Egyptian kings were placed inside pyramids. No one is certain why they chose this unusual building shape, but some scholars think that the sloping sides represent the sun's rays. A total of 35 big pyramids were erected near the Nile River in Egypt. Forty smaller ones were built for queens.

Ten such pyramids stand at Giza. They are located near what is now the capital city of Cairo in Egypt. Three are the largest of all the pyramids. Each was built to house the body of an Egyptian king, or pharaoh. His body was put into a secret chamber in the midst of a confusing maze. He lay surrounded by treasures made of gold.

The pyramids at Giza were built between 2600 and 2500 B.C.E. The largest is called the Great Pyramid. Built for King Khufu, it kept 100,000 workers laboring for 20 years. It is so perfectly proportioned that the largest error between side lengths is less than one percent! It is made of about two million stone blocks. Each one of them had to be placed carefully. And each one weighed two tons! How did they do it before any modern equipment was available? No one knows.

Some people think that a clay called tafla is the answer. Wet tafla is slippery. Using ramps of wet tafla, a large team of men could slide the two-ton blocks up the side of a pyramid. A pole set in a corner of the pyramid would swing the blocks into place. Four such ramps surrounded the pyramid. These ramps were kept wet by workers whose job it was to continually bring water from the Nile River. When the pyramid was complete, the tafla dried out and hardened. Then it was easy to break apart with a pick axe. Others believe there were spiral ramps. A third theory is that levers manipulated the heavy blocks.

When it was built, the Great Pyramid was 481 feet tall. It no longer comes to a perfect point at the top. It has lost about 30 feet from its peak due to sandstorm erosion. Yet it was the tallest structure on Earth for more than 4,300 years. A German cathedral's spire surpassed it in 1880.

Like most of the pyramids, robbers broke into the Great Pyramid. They stole the treasures and even the mummy! Although pyramids were designed to foil thieves, only one tomb has been found intact.

Fit for a King:
The Great Pyramid at Giza

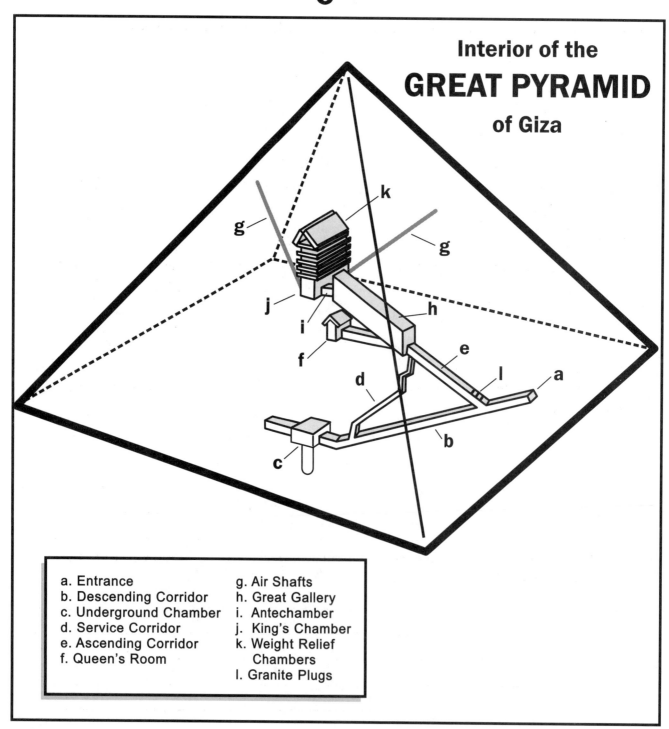

Interior of the
GREAT PYRAMID
of Giza

a. Entrance
b. Descending Corridor
c. Underground Chamber
d. Service Corridor
e. Ascending Corridor
f. Queen's Room
g. Air Shafts
h. Great Gallery
i. Antechamber
j. King's Chamber
k. Weight Relief
   Chambers
l. Granite Plugs

Fit for a King:
The Great Pyramid at Giza

1. The Great Pyramid at Giza is the biggest of how many large Egyptian pyramids?

    a. 10   c. 40

    b. 35   d. 481

2. Talfa is a type of

    a. pyramid.   c. clay.

    b. coffin.   d. lever.

3. What caused the Great Pyramid to lose 30 feet from its peak?

    a. sandstorms   c. hail

    b. snowstorms   d. floods

4. The pyramids are built of huge blocks that were moved into place by levers. True or False? Explain your answer.

_____

_____

_____

5. Why do you think that the passageway to the great gallery of the Great Pyramid is blocked by granite plugs?

_____

_____

_____

_____

6. Should pyramids be open to the public or closed in respect to the final resting place of ancient Egyptian royalty? Defend your stance.

_____

_____

_____

_____

The Great Wall of China

The Great Wall of China is like a gigantic fence built around a nation. The longest manmade structure on Earth, it stretches 4,500 miles along the Chinese border. It is so big it has been seen from the space shuttle! The main part covers about 2,500 miles of northern China. It has eastern and western branches, too. The Wall has an average width of 15 feet and an average height of 30 feet.

The Wall follows the contours of the land as it winds through mountains in the east. Granite blocks form its foundation, and the sides are stone or brick. The inside is filled with hard-packed dirt. The top is paved with bricks and mortar, forming a road used by the workers who built it and the troops who defended it. In the west, the Great Wall runs along a desert's border. Stone and brick were scarce in this dry area, so workers used soil to build this section of the wall. They wet the dirt, formed it, and then pounded it to make it solid.

People built every part of the Great Wall by hand. At one point 1.8 million people labored on it. It was hard work. The workers' living conditions were not good. Many of them died and lie buried within the Wall. This helped the surviving workers since they did not have to spend time and effort burying bodies.

No one is sure of the actual age of the oldest part of the Wall. The Chinese may have built walls along their borders as early as 400 B.C.E. Most people think that Emperor Shi Hanged of the Qin dynasty was the first ruler to make a wall for defense. None of it remains today. Several other emperors also built walls, often by joining new ones with older ones. Some of those walls that were in good shape were added into the Great Wall.

Most of the Great Wall dates from the Ming Dynasty (1368–1644). The emperor ordered its construction in the late 1400s due to Mongol attacks. Like earlier Walls, it protected China from minor attacks, but it did not work against huge invasions. And it did nothing to prevent attacks from the sea. Then cannons were invented, and their use made the Wall obsolete.

The Great Wall was once split into nine sections, or zones. Each zone was guarded by troops. Today the Great Wall no longer offers a means of defense. But it's still valuable to the Chinese. Each year it attracts thousands of tourists and their money. Over time much of it caved in. In the 1980s, the Chinese government repaired the most-visited sections. A popular portion is on Mount Badland near Beijing. This part has towers that once served as lookout posts.

The Great Wall of China

86. Camel train from Mongolia via Nankow Pass, coming through the Great Wall of China. Copyright 1902 by C. H. Graves.

Courtesy of the Library of Congress, "Camel Train from Mongolia . . . . the Great Wall of China 1902," LC-USZ62-56117

The Great Wall of China

1. The Great Wall was built as a

   a. tourist attraction.

   b. defensive measure.

   c. monument to the Ming Dynasty.

   d. burial place for workers.

2. After cannons were invented,

   a. they could blow holes through the Great Wall.

   b. they were added to the top of the Great Wall.

   c. the Great Wall was more useful than ever before.

   d. the Great Wall was made higher.

3. The Japanese were able to invade China because the Great Wall

   a. was crumbling in disrepair.

   b. was never completed.

   c. didn't run along the sea coast.

   d. couldn't withstand a small invasion.

4. Today the Great Wall is an important tourist attraction. True or False? Explain.

_____

_____

_____

5. Did the Great Wall stop traders from traveling across China? How do you know?

_____

_____

_____

_____

6. The Great Wall helped to isolate China from Europe and the Middle East. Was this a good thing? Why?

_____

_____

_____

_____

_____

The Moai on Easter Island

Easter Island lies in the middle of the Pacific Ocean. It is 4,300 miles west of South America and 2,300 miles east of Tahiti. On it stands 600 huge statues, or moai. Some are as tall as three-story buildings. They are carved in the shape of men. Some weigh 90 tons! A few have fallen and lie in ruins.

The Dutch explorer Jacob Roggeveen named the island when he first saw it on Easter Sunday in 1722. He had no idea how people had erected such huge statues. His questions remain unanswered. Who made these statues? How were they built? And why? No one knows for sure.

A Norwegian, Thor Heyerdahl, thought that he had the answers. He said that people left South America on rafts and floated to Easter Island. He saw similarities between the culture of the Incas and the ancient people on the Island. Sweet potatoes grew in both places. Nearly identical spearheads were found in both spots, too. The islanders worshipped Tiki, a white chief. The Incas had a white chief named Kon-Tiki. But he was chased out of Peru and set adrift in the sea. Could he be the same man?

People argued that no one could survive such a trip. Heyerdahl was so determined to prove his theory that he made a risky trip in 1947. He and five others built a crude balsawood raft. They went 4,300 miles across the Pacific Ocean on it! Their nine-log raft, the *Kon-Tiki*, was tied together with hemp rope, just like an ancient one. The men sailed from Peru for 101 days. The hot sun scorched the crew. At one point several of them got washed overboard in a bad storm. Sharks attacked the flimsy raft. The six men landed on an uninhabited island near Tahiti. They proved that people could survive a raft trip. But they hadn't proven that the islanders came from Peru.

Some people discounted Heyerdahl's achievement. His raft used sails. The Incas only had paddles. He also had his raft towed 50 miles out to sea. This way he avoided the currents that would have kept him near Peru. The Incas would have had to fight these currents. Others say that he's got the story backwards. The Polynesians were good sailors. They went to islands like Hawaii and New Zealand. Maybe the spearheads and sweet potatoes came from Polynesians. They sailed to South America and back home again.

The statues may have been built to honor the gods or people's ancestors. Whatever their purpose, the islanders used hand picks to carve the stone from an old volcano. It would have taken years to make one statue. Red stone cylinders rest like crowns on some moai heads. Making and moving these statues and putting cylinders atop them would be hard to do even with modern equipment. That adds to the mystery of Easter Island, which now draws tourists from around the world.

Carbon dating shows that the first moai were built around 900 C.E. Two Easter Islander tribes fought a war around 1680. The winners knocked over some of the moai. Now 15 have been restored.

The Moai on Easter Island

Sign Our Guestbook   Other Resources   Webmaster   Contact Us

Mysterious Easter Island

Who Settled Easter Island?

According to archeologist Thor Heyerdahl, Easter Island was settled in stages by two different races. One group came from Polynesia (islands in the South Pacific Ocean). The other came from Peru in South America. Tools, statues, and legends in both places are alike. However, archeologists attacked Heyerdahl's theory. They accused him of tampering with evidence to make it fit his theory.

The Rapa Nui are the natives living on Easter Island. They look Polynesian, and modern archeologists say that they are pure Polynesian. Hundreds of years ago a group of them left another island and sailed east. They found Easter Island. They had no contact with any other races. That is the official stand of the archaeological community. But new evidence has raised questions.

Around 1563 the ship *San Lesmems* sank near the island of Tahiti. The sailors on this ship were Basques. They lived in parts of Spain and France. Legends say that the survivors made it to shore. The islanders nursed them to health. The Basque men married the women. They had children. Around 1600 either they or their offspring set sail from Tahiti. But no one ever heard from them again.

Tahiti lies 2,000 miles west of Easter Island. The theory states that they landed on Easter Island. They gave up the idea of returning to Europe and stayed there. Recent DNA testing showed that pure-blooded Rapa Nuis have some Basque genes. This disproves the Polynesian-only theory. And it supports the observations made by Jacob Roggeveen, the Dutch "discoverer" of Easter Island. In 1722, he reported a population with both light-skinned and dark-skinned members. Some had red hair and sun-burnt flesh.

Choose a link:

Why did they make
the statues?

How were the
statues made?

How were the
statues moved?

The Moai on Easter Island

1. The Easter Island moai are made of

   a. cement.

   b. hard-packed earth.

   c. sun-dried mud bricks.

   d. volcanic rock.

2. Easter Island is located closest to

   a. Tahiti.

   b. Hawaii.

   c. New Zealand.

   d. Peru.

3. Thor Heyerdahl was born in

   a. Tahiti.

   b. Norway.

   c. Peru.

   d. Easter Island.

4. Jacob Roggeveen believed Thor Heyerdahl's theory of how Easter Island was settled. True or False? Explain.

   _____

   _____

   _____

5. What do most archaeologists think of Thor Heyerdahl and his raft trip?

   _____

   _____

   _____

   _____

   _____

6. Which of the three theories summarized on the web page do you believe tells how Easter Island was settled? Defend your stance.

   _____

   _____

   _____

   _____

   _____

A Monument to Love: The Taj Mahal

The Taj Mahal is the best-known tomb in the world. It is also one of the most lovely and expensive. Taj Mahal means "Crown Palace." The Indian ruler Shah Jahan had it built. He made it for his favorite wife, Mumtaz Mahal. She died in 1629 not long after she had her fourteenth child. As she lay dying, he said he'd build a monument for her that would match her beauty.

Every fact about the Taj Mahal is amazing. It took 1,000 elephants to bring the materials from central Asia to the site. It took 20,000 workers to build it. They labored from 1632 until 1653.

The tomb stands on the bank of the River Yamuna in Agra, India. It is surrounded by vast gardens. They are laid out in geometric patterns. The effect is similar to a beautiful Persian rug. Islamic art often uses such designs because Muslims cannot create images of humans or their god, Allah.

Red sandstone walls enclose gardens that surround the tomb and other structures. There are several watch towers. A mosque (place of worship) and a guest house are closest to the tomb. These buildings are precise mirror images of each other. The main gate has verses from the Koran, the holy book of Islam.

The Taj Mahal itself is made of white marble. It stands on a red sandstone base. At each corner of this base stands a tall, thin prayer tower called a minaret. A dome shaped like an onion rests over the center of the building. Four smaller domes surround it. Verses from the Koran decorate the outer walls. These walls also have geometric and floral designs inlaid with semiprecious gems. These jewels include jasper (red) and agate, which comes in a rainbow of colors. The gems make the walls sparkle at night when they catch the light of the moon.

The tomb's central room has two monuments. The bodies of Shah Jahan and his wife lie in a vault below them. Each one has elaborate carvings and inlaid gems. As sunlight filters through a carved marble screen, the gems glow. Tourists must stay behind this screen.

The Taj Mahal is one of the eight Wonders of the World. But now it is being damaged by acid rain which wears away the marble and sandstone. In 2006, a monkey leaped onto a flower vase carved atop a sandstone turret on the main gate. Weakened by time and acid rain, the vase crashed to the ground. Fortunately no one was hurt.

A Monument to Love: The Taj Mahal

Courtesy of the Library of Congress, " The Taj Mahal," LC-USZ62-29053

Hi, Mom! Dad and I are having a great time in India. We spent the day at the Taj Mahal. Isn't it beautiful? Every detail is perfect. I was disappointed that there are no portraits of the king who built it or the queen he made it for. It would be nice to know what they looked like. You'd love the gardens—they're awesome! Wish you were here. Love ya, Maria

Edelia Lopez
65 Harrington Terrace
Westminster, CA 92863

A Monument to Love: The Taj Mahal

1. What is damaging the Taj Mahal?

   a. global warming

   b. flooding from the River Yamuna

   c. acid rain

   d. the sun's ultraviolet rays

2. The Taj Mahal is made of

   a. semiprecious jewels.

   b. granite.

   c. sandstone.

   d. marble.

3. The Taj Mahal took

   a. about 10 years to build.

   b. more than 20 years to build.

   c. 30 years to build.

   d. 50 years to build.

4. Shah Jahan and Mumtaz Mahal were Muslims. True or False? Explain.

_____

_____

_____

5. Why are no images of Shah Jahan and Mumtaz Mahal included in the Taj Mahal?

_____

_____

_____

_____

_____

6. Would you like to visit the Taj Mahal? Why or why not?

_____

_____

_____

_____

_____

The Panama Canal

For hundreds of years, sailors wanted a faster way to get their ships from the Pacific Ocean to the Atlantic Ocean. A ship sailing from San Francisco to New York covered 15,100 miles. Why? To get from the Pacific to the Atlantic, it had to go all the way around Cape Horn at the tip of South America. The trip would be 9,000 miles shorter if a canal connected the oceans.

The French were the first to try to build such a canal. They chose Panama, a narrow country in Central America. This nation is just 40 miles wide. In 1880, the French started to build a canal across it. But their plans failed, and hundreds of men died from malaria and yellow fever. In all, 22,000 men died, many from landslides while digging a pass through the mountains. France gave up.

In 1903 President Theodore Roosevelt gained the rights to build a canal through Panama. He hired an engineer to lead the project. General George Goethals' job was to find answers to the problems that had stopped the French. Where the land rose, the ships had to rise as well. Where the land dipped, the ships had to go down, too. So Goethals and his team made three sets of water-filled chambers, or locks. These locks raise and lower the water level for the ships. The locks were built in pairs. That way ships could move in both directions at the same time. One ship can be in one lock going east while another ship is in the other lock going west. Small electric locomotives run on tracks beside the locks. They guide the ships.

Large ships completely fill the locks. There may be just four inches between the hull and the sides! The size of the locks limit the ships that can use the Canal. Oil supertankers and U.S. Navy aircraft carriers are too big.

At the time the Canal was built, Panama had some of the deadliest diseases on Earth. So Goethals hired a doctor. He wanted to keep the workers alive. The doctor could not cure malaria. But he did eliminate yellow fever, which reduced the deaths. Still, by the end of the project, nearly 6,000 men had died.

About 40,000 workers labored for a decade to build the Canal. They used steam shovels and dredges. They cut through thick jungles, steep hills, and swamps. The Panama Canal is considered one of the greatest engineering achievements ever. It cost the United States more than $380 million to build. It held ownership through 1999. Then it gave the Canal to Panama.

On August 15, 1914, the first ship, the *Alcon*, sailed from one ocean to the other. It took just 15 hours. Now 12,000 ships pass through the Canal each year. They carry about 260 million tons of cargo. Panama earns millions of dollars from the tolls charged to use the Canal.

The Panama Canal

This diagram shows the lock system of the Panama Canal.

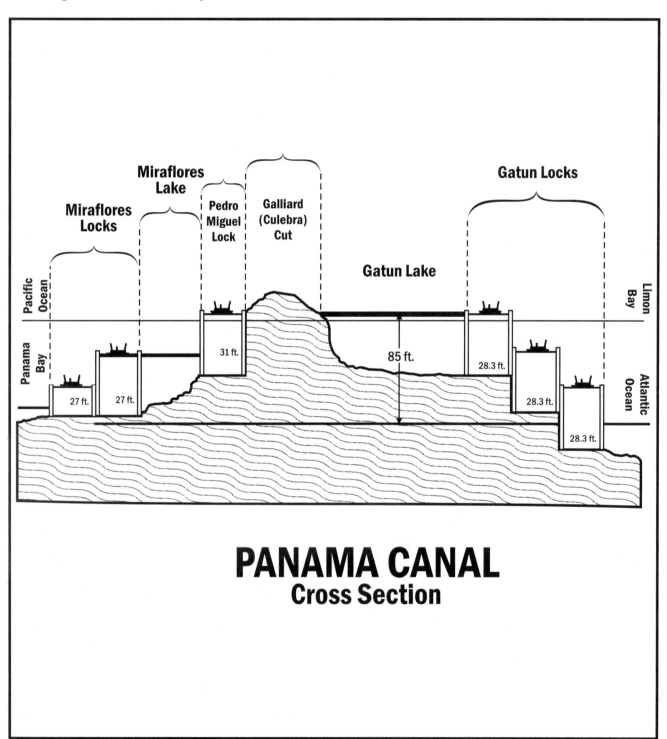

PANAMA CANAL
Cross Section

The Panama Canal

1. The Panama Canal reduced the length of a ship's trip from New York to San Francisco by

    a. 4,600 miles.   c. 9,000 miles.

    b. 6,100 miles.   d. 15,100 miles

2. The nation of Panama was chosen for the canal because

    a. the United States controlled
        the nation.   c. it was the narrowest land area
                                            between the Pacific and Atlantic Oceans.

    b. the French owned the nation.   d. it already had a system of locks.

3. The locks shown in the diagram look most like

    a. water-filled stairways.   c. islands.

    b. skyscrapers.   d. mountains.

4. The Panama Canal passes through three lakes. True or False? Explain.

_____

_____

_____

5. What are the names of the Panama Canal's locks? Why were they built in pairs?

_____

_____

_____

_____

_____

6. Should the Panama Canal continue to charge a toll to the ships that use it? Defend your stance.

_____

_____

_____

_____

The Three Gorges Dam

The Three Gorges Dam spans the Yangtze River in China. It is the biggest hydroelectric dam on Earth. It is 610 feet tall. It stretches 1 ⅓ miles across the width of the world's third longest river.

Work on the Dam began in 1993. About 40,000 workers worked 24 hours a day to build it. Water backed up behind it, forming a new lake called a reservoir. This reservoir began to fill on June 1, 2003. It is almost 400 miles long.

Electrical generation began two months later. The next year boats started going through the Dam's locks. The locks let ships bypass the Dam. This keeps the river navigable. Construction ended in 2006. However, the Dam would not operate at full capacity until 2009.

The Three Gorges Dam caused a lot of debate. Supporters stressed the humane and economic benefits. The Dam offers both flood control and hydroelectric power. Before, huge floods occurred at least once a decade. Hundreds of thousands died each time. Now such floods should be reduced to one per century.

Also, China needed more electrical power. Prior to the dam, power shortages were a fact of life. Blackouts were common. They happened often in cities in the summer. The dam may generate up to 11 percent of the nation's electricity. As an added bonus, this power is clean. Hydropower does not pollute the air. Why? Water flows through the dam. It makes a turbine turn, just like a water wheel on a mill. The turbine's spinning makes electricity.

Critics disliked how the dam's reservoir flooded 1,200 towns. More than 1.2 million people had to leave their homes. Most did not want to go. The government made them. Some of the most fertile land in China was flooded. The land to which the farmers moved was not as good for growing crops. The water covered 16 archaeological sites, too. Ancient buildings—some 3,000 years old—now stand deep underwater. Worst of all, the only sites of the Ba, an ancient people who lived in China about 4,000 years ago, were lost.

The effects on the environment upset many people. Thousands of acres of forest were drowned. Scientists trapped the wild animals living in the area. They moved them to new places. But not every animal could be found and removed. Many animals drowned in the rising water.

The Three Gorges Dam

This cut away diagram shows how the Three Gorges Dam makes electrical power.

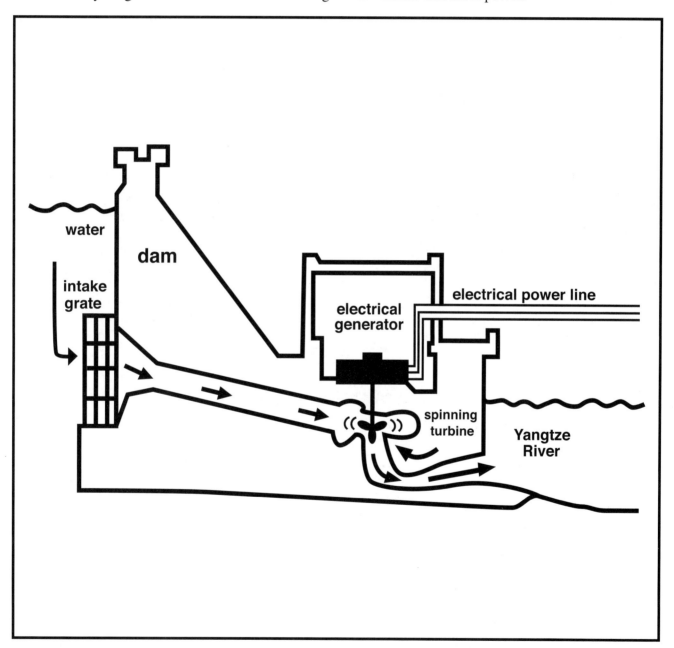

The Three Gorges Dam

1. What is one positive impact the Three Gorges Dam has had on China?

    a. It generates clean electrical power.

    b. It shortens the time it takes for a ship to go the entire length of the Yangtze River.

    c. It caused 1.2 million people to find new homes.

    d. It left archaeological sites under water.

2. A navigable river is one on which boats

    a. can reach the sea.

    b. often sink due to underwater hazards.

    c. can't travel.

    d. can travel.

3. You can tell that all of the flooded villages, forests, and farms were located within

    a. 1 1/3 miles of the Three Gorges Dam.

    b. 400 miles of the Three Gorges Dam.

    c. 1,200 miles of the Three Gorges Dam.

    d. 4,000 miles of the Three Gorges Dam.

4. From the lake behind the dam, the water flows by gravity to the turbines that generate electricity. True or False? Explain.

_____

_____

_____

5. Look at the diagram. Why is there a grate over the water intake?

_____

_____

_____

_____

6. Should the Three Gorges Dam have been built? Defend your stance.

_____

_____

_____

_____

Mount Tambora, A Violent Volcano

After years of silence, a volcano awoke in 1815. It stood on the island of Sumbawa in Indonesia. Mount Tambora had formed over millions of years. Lava had flowed up from the sea floor until the volcano towered 13,000 feet above the sea. Yet it had stood quietly for so long that thick forests covered its slopes.

On April 5 the mountain made some noises. The next day some light ash came from the cone. The people living on the island did not even realize where it came from! Clouds blocked the top of their mountain. They thought it was from another volcano on a nearby island. Over the next few days the ground trembled. Then, on the evening of April 10, the eruption began. Flames shot out of the cone while lightning flashed above it. Lava flowed down its sides. Volcanic bombs the size of a human fist rained down. Wild waves claimed huge chunks of the shore as the land sank into the sea. Seaside towns were suddenly 18 feet under water. For three days the sun's light was blocked, and the people could not tell day from night.

Mount Tambora erupted on and off for three months in the worst volcanic disaster in recorded history. The huge amount of lava, ash, and deadly gases killed every plant on Sumbawa and all the surrounding islands. Nobody dared go near the island until August. They were shocked by what they found. Before 12,000 people had called Sumbawa home. Just 40 had survived.

In the years that followed many more people died because the volcano had destroyed crops. People had no food to eat. Dust and ash had tainted the water supply, too. People grew weak and fell ill. About 92,000 died in all. Back then there was no Red Cross or other relief groups to help them.

The eruption also caused trouble for people living on the other side of the world. In 1816, the northeastern part of the U.S. and Canada had the "year without a summer." The weather was strange all summer. It snowed in June, and every month had a killing frost. Farmers planted crops several times, but every time they died. The ruined crops stretched all the way to Virginia.

No one knew what was going on. Now we know that the volcano threw so much dust and ash into the air that it blocked the sunlight. The sun's rays could not get through, and this kept the northern part of North America colder than usual. It took a year for most of the ash to fall to the ground. Then temperatures returned to normal.

Mount Tambora still stands, although now it is just 9,000 feet high. It has been quiet for almost 200 years. But it can awaken at any time. Fortunately the mountain is now monitored by scientific equipment. This may give people more warning and a chance to escape.

Mount Tambora, a Violent Volcano

Major Volcanic Eruptions (through 2006)

Year	Volcano	Nation	Deaths
79	Mount Vesuvius	Italy	20,000
1631	Mount Vesuvius	Italy	3,500
1669	Mount Etna	Italy	20,000
1783	Mount Skaptar	Iceland	9,000
1792	Mount Mayuyama	Japan	15,000
1815	Mount Tambora	Indonesia	70,000+
1822	Galunggung	Indonesia	4,000
1883	Krakatoa	Indonesia	36,000
1902	Mount Pelée	West Indies	30,000+
1919	Mount Kelud	Indonesia	5,000
1951	Mount Lamington	New Guinea	3,000
1985	Nevado del Ruiz	Colombia	23,000
1991	Mount Pinatubo	Philippines	1,200

Mount Tambora, a Violent Volcano

1. How long was the island of Sumbawa in complete darkness?

    a. three hours

    b. three days

    c. three weeks

    d. three months

2. Mount Tambora's eruption caused the "year without a summer" in

    a. Sumbawa.

    b. Canada.

    c. Indonesia.

    d. all around the world.

3. Why didn't anyone go to Sumbawa until August?

    a. because they were too preoccupied with the fact that there was no summer

    b. because most people were too afraid of seeing dead bodies

    c. because the volcano kept erupting on and off from April to July

    d. because the people living in the area believed that the island was under a curse until August

4. The long-term problems caused by the Mount Tambora eruption killed more people than the eruption itself. True or False? Explain.

_____

_____

_____

5. In terms of deadly volcanoes, what nation is the worst in which to live? Is Mount Tambora in that nation? Use facts from the chart in your answer.

_____

_____

_____

_____

_____

6. Are the people living at the base of Mount Tambora today in as much danger as the people in 1815? Defend your stance.

_____

_____

_____

_____

_____

The Great Irish Famine

Some disasters begin so quietly that at first no one realizes their seriousness. This was true of the Great Irish Famine. A *famine* is a period of widespread starvation. Between 1845 and 1851, 1.5 million Irish died. It all started with blight. This fungus would kill a healthy potato plant in several days. Then the potatoes could not be eaten. And potatoes were the only food that the poor had.

Ireland is called the Emerald Isle. Although it is as far north as Moscow, Russia, its climate is mild. Why? The Gulf Stream is an ocean current. It carries warm water and air from the Caribbean to Ireland. The cool, damp climate is good for growing potatoes. But it is also ideal for blight.

Religion played a part in the tragedy that unfolded. Protestants owned the land. The Roman Catholic farmers were their tenants. They grew wheat and oats in big fields. The money from these crops paid their rent. They also had small plots on which to raise potatoes for themselves. Many other people just worked in the fields. They lived in tiny mud huts and had gardens in which they grew enough potatoes to survive. Unlike grains, potatoes could not be stored for years. Each year's crop fed the people until the next harvest.

Although Ireland was part of the United Kingdom, there had been religious tension between the two islands for centuries. Why? Most of the British were Protestants. Most of the Irish were Roman Catholics. The British did little to help the Irish during the famine. They simply did not seem to care about their suffering. Irish farmers and workers had little to eat. Many of the poor sold all that they owned to buy food. When that ran out, they starved. British landlords made hundreds of thousands of people leave their homes and farms when they couldn't pay their rent. Eviction was a death sentence. Then people slowly starved to death. Some caring landlords paid for tickets for their tenants to take a ship to North America.

Other crops did well during the blight. But the landlords exported them! The year that the greatest number of people starved was 1847. That same year 4,000 shiploads of food left Ireland for England or Scotland. At last the British government set up a public works program. It hired people to build roads and bridges so that they could buy food. But most could not earn enough to feed a family. Soup kitchens could not keep up with the demand. Diseases killed the weakened people, too. So many people were dying so fast that survivors ran out of caskets. People stacked corpses like logs in mass graves.

Although things improved in 1851, another famine struck Ireland in 1879. Between starvation and people fleeing, just half of the Irish population was left by 1900. Many blamed the British government for its indifference. In 1997, the British prime minister formally apologized for the nation's lack of action.

The Great Irish Famine

Courtesy of the Library of Congress,
"The Herald of Relief from America," LC-USZ62-103220

Irish immigrants spread word of the disaster upon their arrival in America. Relief groups soon organized all over the nation. Members of the Cherokee Choctaw tribe made a donation of $710. That's the same as $100,000 in today's money.

One of the groups who helped the Irish the most was the Quakers (Society of Friends). They raised money to pay for people's ship tickets to America. They also sent flour, rice, biscuits, and Indian meal to the starving Irish.

The Great Irish Famine

1. The Great Irish Famine lasted for

    a. 6 years.

    b. 10 years

    c. 15 years.

    d. 50 years.

2. Blight is a kind of

    a. bacteria.

    b. virus.

    c. potato.

    d. fungus.

3. Why was eviction a death sentence to the tenant farmers?

    a. because it made the blight spread faster

    b. because then the people had to go to America or Canada

    c. because the people no longer had shelter or any way to get food

    d. because the British government refused to let the starving people go to Great Britain

4. Religious issues helped to make this disaster worse. True or False? Explain.

    _____

    _____

    _____

5. *Harper's Weekly* was published in New York City. What message was the magazine cover trying to send to its readers?

    _____

    _____

    _____

    _____

6. Do you think that the British improved in their response to the Irish famine that occurred in 1879–1880? Defend your stance.

    _____

    _____

    _____

    _____

Washed Away in the Johnstown Flood

In 1889, Johnstown, Pennsylvania was a busy steel-mill city. About 30,000 people lived there. On May 31, 1889, they suffered a tragedy that shocked the nation.

Johnstown stood at the fork of two rivers. Since people had built factories along the river, its banks had narrowed. Minor floods had occurred after heavy rains. On that fateful rainy day, the people of Johnstown did have some warning of danger. A small dam in Stony Creek broke about noon. It swept lumber into the river. Boards floated through the center of town. A few people who saw that left the city. They were the lucky ones.

Fourteen miles upstream, the old South Fork Dam held back a lake on a hillside 450 feet above the city. The South Fork Hunting and Fishing Club had built it. The earthen dam had not been well-kept. On May 31, due to the heavy rain, the club's president sent men to shore up the dam. The workers reported that despite their efforts the dam wouldn't hold. At 3:10 P.M. he sent a telegram to warn the people in Johnstown. But in those days there was no way to quickly get the word out to every home.

At 4:07 P.M. the dam burst, sending a 60-foot-high wall of water rushing into the valley below. Twenty million tons of water roared at 40 miles per hour toward the city. The water swept up everything in its path, including a whole freight train. It crashed through a wire-making plant and a lumberyard. Hundreds of homes sank into the water. Some people became tangled in coils of barbed wire. Others were hit by the logs. A few grabbed hold of things in the churning water and used them as rafts. Huge oil tanks spilled, coating everything in oil.

The city's old stone bridge stood fast. It held back the crushing weight of all the debris. When darkness fell, hundreds of people were still trapped near the bridge. Rescuers pulled people from the wreckage. But then the oily water and debris caught fire. At least 80 people died in the flames.

People rushed to Johnstown to help. The rescuers took home 200 orphans. The flood killed 2,209 people and injured many more. Hundreds of people—including whole families—were never found. It took five years to clean up and rebuild the city. The South Fork Hunting and Fishing Club did not pay for any of the damage.

Washed Away
in the Johnstown Flood

The New York Times June 3, 1889 The Desolated Valley

Victims to be Counted by Thousands

The Survivors Homeless and Starving

Terrible Scenes Among the Ruins of Johnstown

The area of disaster from the floods is extended considerably over what was originally reported. Organized efforts to provide food and shelter for the homeless thousands that are now exposed to the elements are earnestly called for.

The cause of the calamity, it is admitted by the President of the South Fork Fishing Club, was the weakness of the dam alone. The frailty of the dam and the tremendous pressure of water behind it was the only cause of the catastrophe.

Courtesy of the Library of Congress, "Johnstown Disaster—fire at the bridge," LC-USZ62-98442

The New York Times June 7, 1889 Peril After the Flood

From Johnstown Down to the Ohio Valley
Contaminated Water and Death-Bearing Odors

The Sanitary Authorities Hampered by a Lack of Disinfectants and Too Few Skilled Assistants

Rapid Work in Removing the Wreckage—Still Finding and Burying Bodies

Dr. Lee of the State Board of Health and his associates made a house-to-house inspection of the upper part of the city today. In many houses 13 and 14 people were found living in a single room with the windows tightly closed to keep out the stench of decaying bodies and animals.

The supply of disinfectants is inadequate. The supply on hand has been exhausted, and Dr. Lee has telegraphed to the Surgeon General of the United States for more. He replied that all the disinfectants available, three (train) carloads, had been sent and were on the way. Yet this will not be one-tenth of the quantity required. Another necessity for disinfection is tar. The odor which would arise from burning tar would, according to Dr. Lee, be of value to the hill dwellers, as well as to the residents of the destroyed city.

That the danger of the poisoned water is understood in Pittsburgh is evidenced this morning by the warning of the President of the local Board of Health, instructing the citizens that they should filter and boil water before it is used. Already the Allegheny River water is unfit to drink.

Johnstown Pennsylvania Information Source Online. "New York Times Articles about the Great Flood."
http://www.johnstownpa.com/History/hist30.html

Washed Away
in the Johnstown Flood

1. The huge amount of debris being swept down the river was stopped by

    a. the old stone bridge in Johnstown.

    b. a mountain near a sharp bend in the river.

    c. big concrete barricades.

    d. another dam in Pittsburgh.

2. Rescuers took home orphans because these children

    a. didn't want to live in Johnstown.

    b. had not survived the flood.

    c. didn't want to find their families.

    d. had lost their parents and needed someone to take care of them.

3. People trapped in the raging floodwaters tried to

    a. swim to the shore.

    b. grab hold of debris to stay afloat.

    c. climb the rescue ladders dropped by helicopters.

    d. coat themselves in oil to keep warm in the cold water.

4. The people of Johnstown had some warning of the possibility of a flood disaster. True or False? Explain your answer.

    _____

    _____

    _____

5. Why were disinfectants needed after the flood?

    _____

    _____

    _____

    _____

    _____

6. Should the South Fork Hunting and Fishing Club have paid for some or all of the clean up costs after the flood? Defend your stance.

    _____

    _____

    _____

    _____

    _____

The Great San Francisco Earthquake and Fire

A century ago, San Francisco was a busy port town. But early on the morning of April 18, 1906, while most of its citizens were still asleep, it suffered a great disaster. A huge earthquake measuring 8.3 on the Richter scale shook the city and surrounding area.

The strongest shaking lasted just one minute. It ran 296 miles along the San Andreas fault line. The ground rolled, like waves in the sea. Some sections of fences moved 8.5 feet from where they'd been placed. This didn't cause bad damage or kill many people in the rural areas. Few people lived there, and they had small homes surrounded by open spaces. But in San Francisco, houses slid off their foundations. Some fell on the houses next door, causing a domino effect. Streetcar and railroad tracks twisted. Buildings collapsed, and streets cracked. Electrical wires fell to the ground.

Gas mains blew up. Fallen lamps and stoves started more fires. Most of the city's buildings were wooden. They provided fuel for the fire. The city's water pipes were damaged. The water spilled out of the broken pipes into the ground. So the firemen could not use the water to fight the fires. The blaze spread for three days. Makeshift hospitals and morgues were set up in homes. But they had to keep moving to stay ahead of the flames. After a while the dead were abandoned. It was more important to keep moving the injured.

The desperate firemen began dynamiting blocks of buildings. They hoped to create a wide firebreak that the flames could not jump. Eventually this did stop the fire. But the center of the city—more than 3,000 acres—lay blackened and smoldering.

When the smoke cleared, over 28,000 buildings had been ruined. Even the inside of brick buildings had been destroyed. About 3,000 people had died. And nearly a quarter million were homeless. It remains one of the worst disasters in U.S. history.

Another strong earthquake struck the city again in 1989. Buildings and highways were damaged, but this time just 63 people died. The modern buildings had been designed to withstand strong earthquakes.

The Great San Francisco Earthquake and Fire

PROCLAMATION
BY THE MAYOR

The Federal Troops, the members of the Regular Police Force and all Special Police Officers have been authorized by me to KILL any and all persons found engaged in Looting or in the Commission of Any Other Crime.

I have directed all the Gas and Electric Lighting Co.'s not to turn on Gas or Electricity until I order them to do so. You may therefore expect the city to remain in darkness for an indefinite time.

I request all citizens to remain at home from darkness until daylight every night until order is restored.

I WARN all Citizens of the danger of fire from Damaged or Destroyed Chimneys, Broken or Leaking Gas Pipes or Fixtures, or any like cause.

E. E. SCHMITZ, Mayor

Dated, April 18, 1906.

ALTVATER PRINT, MISSION AND 220 STS.

Virtual Museum of the City of San Francisco.
Mayor Eugene Schmitz's Famed Shoot-to-Kill Order – April 18, 1906.
http://www.sfmuseum.org/1906.2/killproc.html

The Great San Francisco Earthquake and Fire

1. What did the San Francisco firemen use to fight the fire?

    a. water   c. dirt barricades

    b. dynamite   d. foam fire extinguishers

2. Why did the people have to leave the dead bodies behind?

    a. They only had one hour to get out of the city before it was completely destroyed.

    b. They didn't care about the dead bodies.

    c. No one could find the dead bodies.

    d. They had to keep moving wounded people in order to stay ahead of the fire.

3. Why were gas and electric services shut off in San Francisco?

    a. Gas and electricity weren't needed anymore.

    b. No one could afford to pay for these services after the earthquake.

    c. Gas would add fuel to the fires and electricity could cause sparks that started more fires.

    d. The mayor wanted people to use their fireplaces instead.

4. After the disaster, even many brick buildings that were still standing had been ruined. True or False? Explain.

_____

_____

_____

5. Who was E. E. Schmitz and why did he request that citizens stay home every night?

_____

_____

_____

_____

_____

6. Do you think that it was wise for San Francisco's mayor to authorize the killing of anyone caught committing a crime after the disaster? Defend your stance.

_____

_____

_____

_____

The Sinking of the *Lusitania*

On May 1, 1915, the British ship *Lusitania* set sail. It left New York heading for England. On board were the captain, 702 crew, and 1,257 passengers. At that time sailing was the only way to cross the ocean.

New York reporters had called this the "Last Voyage of the *Lusitania*." Ten days before, a notice was printed in U.S. newspapers. It stated that Germany would sink any enemy ship. World War I had begun nine months before. Great Britain, Germany, and other European nations were fighting. The Germans had submarines. They had orders to torpedo any British ship. Germany wanted to stop war supplies from reaching Great Britain. Even a passenger ship might hold food for the troops.

The *Lusitania* was one of the biggest passenger ships in the world. It had the typical cargo carried on an ocean liner. But it also held more than 4,200 cases of ammunition. The ship's trip across the Atlantic Ocean went well until May 7, when the ship neared the Irish coast. In recent weeks German subs had sunk hundreds of merchant ships in the area. Most people onboard didn't know this. They wondered why they could see no other ships. Irish ships were supposed to escort them. But they never showed up. Instead, a German sub fired a torpedo. It tore a hole in the ship and caused an explosion.

Many died instantly. Others tried to get into lifeboats. But the ship rolled back and forth. The lifeboats crashed against its sides. Some of them smashed into jagged pieces. Others could not be released. Just six of the 48 lifeboats made it into the water. A second blast threw hundreds of people into the sea. The ship sank in just 18 minutes. The captain and other survivors grabbed debris. The debris kept them afloat until help arrived hours later.

About 1,200 people died; 128 of them were Americans. President Woodrow Wilson made a formal protest. The German ruler said that it was an error. After that, Germany did not attack passenger ships near Great Britain for almost two years. But Americans were outraged. The sinking of the *Lusitania* was one of the reasons that the United States joined the war in April 1917.

By international law, its military cargo made the *Lusitania* a valid target. But it was years after the war had ended before anyone admitted to its cargo.

The Sinking of the *Lusitania*

This notice appeared in the *New York Times* about one week before the *Lusitania*'s departure from New York City. The notice appeared on the same page that advertised the *Lusitania*'s scheduled trip.

NOTICE!

TRAVELLERS intending to embark on the Atlantic voyage are reminded that a state of war exists between Germany and her allies and Great Britain and her allies; that the zone of war includes the waters adjacent to the British Isles; that, in accordance with formal notice given by the Imperial German Government, vessels flying the flag of Great Britain, or any of her allies, are liable to destruction in those waters and that travellers sailing in the war zone on ships of Great Britain or her allies do so at their own risk.

IMPERIAL GERMAN EMBASSY
WASHINGTON, D. C.,   APRIL 22, 1915

ij61

The Sinking of the *Lusitania*

1. How many Americans died on the *Lusitania*?

   a. 48   c. 1,072

   b. 128   d. 1,200

2. How long did it take for the *Lusitania* to sink?

   a. 6 minutes   c. 48 minutes

   b. 18 minutes   d. more than an hour

3. What was hidden on the *Lusitania*?

   a. ammunition   c. soldiers

   b. passengers   d. food

4. The Irish ships that were to escort the *Lusitania* did not meet the ship. True or False? Explain.

_____

_____

_____

5. What was the purpose of the notice the German ambassador had printed in the *New York Times*?

_____

_____

_____

6. Was the notice the German ambassador had printed in the *New York Times* a clear enough civilian warning to justify the attack on the *Lusitania*? Defend your stance.

_____

_____

_____

_____

_____

The Wrath of Hurricane Katrina

Hurricane Katrina was one of the worst storms ever to strike the United States. It formed in the Caribbean Sea. On August 25, 2005, the storm grazed the tip of Florida. It grew stronger as it swirled across the Gulf of Mexico. It made landfall near the Louisiana-Mississippi border on the morning of August 29.

The day before it reached land, weather forecasters said that the storm's track was headed for New Orleans, Louisiana. This city lies below sea level. Concrete barriers called levees surround it. They are there to prevent flooding. As the storm bore down on them, people were told to get out of the city. But many of the poor and elderly had no way to leave.

Hurricane Katrina's high winds and giant waves wiped out parts of Louisiana, Mississippi, and Alabama. A giant wall of water called a storm surge smashed onto shore. In Biloxi and Gulfport, Mississippi, this surge was 29 feet high. Much of both of these cities vanished. The remaining buildings were ruined.

New Orleans had the worst loss of life. Four of its levees broke. As a result, 80 percent of the city flooded. In some places the water was 20 feet deep. It covered the roofs of one-story homes. This water was filled with sewage, gas, chemicals, dead animals, mud, and debris.

For a week after the storm, the news showed images of hundreds of people stuck on roofs while dead people floated by in the flooded streets. Hundreds were stranded in the hot sun on highway overpasses. More than 20,000 people were inside the city's sports stadium and a convention center. No one had drinking water or electricity. The situation was bad in hospitals and nursing homes. To keep seriously ill people breathing, nurses had to work ventilators by hand 24 hours a day.

Rescue teams worked day and night. But some survivors caused trouble. Robbers used boats to move through the city and break into stores and homes. Someone even shot at nurses trying to move patients out of the hospital!

It took a week to bus everyone out of the city. They went to shelters in other places. Even so, a month passed before everyone had a roof over his or her head. About half a million people left the city. The storm had left many of them without a home or a job. They decided not to come back.

Hurricane Katrina killed more than 1,700 people. It left hundreds of thousands homeless. It took billions of dollars and many years to restore the area.

The Wrath of Hurricane Katrina

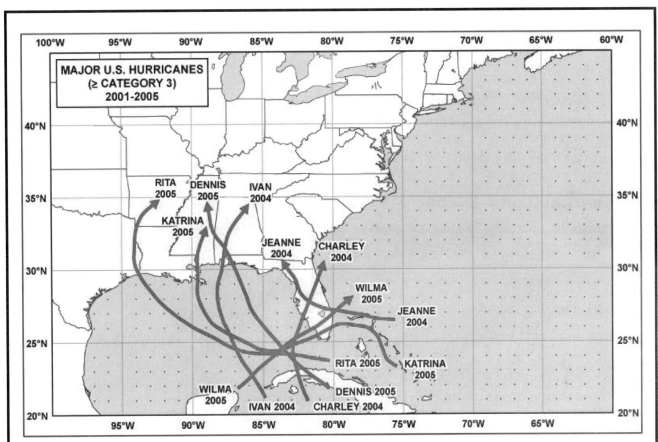

Figure 16. Landfalling United States major hurricanes (stronger than or equal to a category 3) during the period 2001-2005.

National Weather Service National Hurricane Center web site, "Major U.S. Hurricanes 2001-2005"
http://www.nhc.noaa.gov/gifs/DC_16_2001-2005.jpg

The Wrath of Hurricane Katrina

1. Which state was not affected by Hurricane Katrina?

a. Mississippi   c. Georgia

b. Alabama   d. Florida

2. Hurricane Katrina caused the most deaths in

a. Biloxi.   c. Gulfport.

b. New Orleans.   d. the Gulf of Mexico.

3. Ventilators are used to

a. maintain a person's heartbeat.

b. monitor a person's vital signs (heartbeat, breathing, blood pressure).

c. help a patient to breathe.

d. prevent a patient from choking.

4. Hurricane Katrina formed in the Gulf of Mexico. True or False? Explain.

_____

_____

_____

5. Look at the map. Between 2001 and 2005, which year had the most strong hurricanes? Did Hurricane Katrina strike during that year?

_____

_____

_____

_____

_____

6. Should New Orleans have been rebuilt? Defend your stance.

_____

_____

_____

_____

_____

The Unsung Heroes of Fort Mifflin

Few Americans have heard of Fort Mifflin. Yet without it and the men who fought there, there may not have been a United States of America.

The British built Fort Mifflin from 1771 to 1774. It stood on Mud Island in the Delaware River. It was surrounded by a moat. The inside of the fort lay below river level. This made it prone to flooding. It also made it hard to prevent water-borne diseases from sewage.

The Revolutionary War began in April, 1775. Fort Mifflin fell into the hands of the American patriots. On September 27, 1777, the British marched into Philadelphia, Pennsylvania. At that time it was the new nation's capital. The colonial government fled to New York City.

Before the long, cold winter began, the British troops holding the capital needed supplies. Ships planned to bring them food, medicine, warm clothing, and ammunition. They would sail up the Delaware River. But Fort Mifflin stood between them and their troops.

The men within Fort Mifflin were some of the bravest of the Revolution. They knew that they had to stop the ships. They also knew that doing so would probably cost them their lives. In mid October, the British ships opened fire on the little fort. Fort Mifflin had just ten cannons. But it fought back. However, by October 29, the Americans were already running low on ammunition. Constant drizzle caused flooding. Sewage backed up into the fort. Many men fell ill. But the troops at Fort Mifflin did not give up.

The British felt desperate. The Delaware River would freeze. Then they could not reach Philadelphia with the supplies. On November 10, three British ships aimed 158 cannons at Fort Mifflin. It was the first of a 42-day assault. The cannons pummeled the fort 24 hours a day! It was the longest bombardment ever on the North American continent.

The men within the fort held fast. But it was an awful ordeal. They were cold, hungry, sick, and lacked supplies. By Christmas Eve, the fort was totally ruined. The remaining men had orders to leave. Few of the fort's defenders had survived. Yet their sacrifice changed the course of history. They had held up the British until the river froze. Some of the British troops in Philadelphia had to leave. They went to the warmer southern colonies.

Meanwhile George Washington pulled together the Continental Army. He did this in Valley Forge just 20 miles from Philadelphia. For six months, his generals trained the men. They emerged a group of soldiers capable of winning the war.

The Unsung Heroes of Fort Mifflin

Fort Mifflin was restored and used again during the Civil War. Now it is a national historic site. This is a diagram of the fort as it would appear today looking down from above.

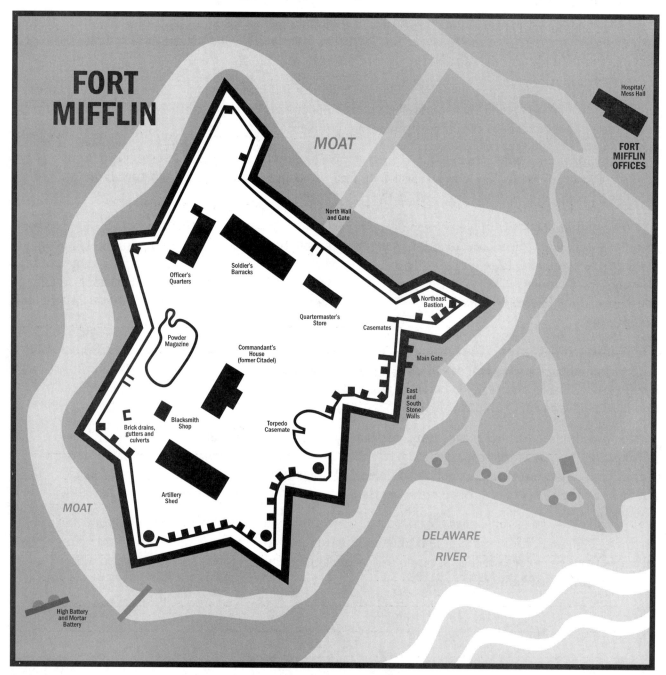

FORT MIFFLIN

Hospital/ Mess Hall

FORT MIFFLIN OFFICES

MOAT

North Wall and Gate

Soldier's Barracks

Officer's Quarters

Northeast Bastion

Quartermaster's Store

Casemates

Powder Magazine

Commandant's House (former Citadel)

Main Gate

East and South Stone Walls

Blacksmith Shop

Brick drains, gutters and culverts

Torpedo Casemate

Artillery Shed

MOAT

DELAWARE RIVER

High Battery and Mortar Battery

The Unsung Heroes of Fort Mifflin

1. In early September 1777, the capital of the United States was

    a. Fort Mifflin.   c. New York City.

    b. Washington, D.C.   d. Philadelphia.

2. Who built Fort Mifflin?

    a. Native Americans   c. the British

    b. American patriots   d. the French

3. Although Fort Mifflin was destroyed, its soldiers had won an important victory because they had

    a. sunk all of the British ships in the Delaware River.   c. made all of the British troops abandon Philadelphia.

    b. kept the British ships occupied until the Delaware River froze.   d. sent Washington the supplies he needed at Valley Forge.

4. The British troops in Philadelphia lacked the supplies necessary to attack Washington's troops at Valley Forge. True or False? Explain.

_____

_____

_____

5. What was the purpose of the moat around Fort Mifflin?

_____

_____

_____

_____

_____

6. Was it wise to build Fort Mifflin with its interior below the river level? Defend your stance.

_____

_____

_____

_____

_____

The Continental Army's Winter at Valley Forge

When the British marched into the patriots' capital on September 27, 1777, the Continental Congress had to flee. It went to New York City. General George Washington hated to leave Philadelphia in British hands. But he had no choice. The Continental Army was not ready to make a move against them. Washington's army of 12,000 men came from 11 of the 13 colonies*. But most were untrained in battle. Many had inadequate clothes and guns. Washington needed time to regroup. He chose to spend the winter in Valley Forge, Pennsylvania. His troops started to set up camp on December 19, 1777.

Washington knew that he had to get his men under shelter fast. He put them into teams of 12. He told them to build log cabins. The men had to cut, haul, and place the logs. Washington gave a $12 reward to the team in each regiment who made a solid cabin in the least time. The men built a total of 2,000 huts. The officers lived in nearby homes. But this doesn't mean that the owners gladly shared their homes. Many wanted to stay out of the war. Some even sympathized with the British.

The people of Connecticut supported their troops. The men from that state had the best supplies of all the troops in Valley Forge. They were put on patrol to keep the encampment from attack. The men from North Carolina had the least supplies. Many of them were barefoot! They kept busy doing inside chores. They cleaned guns and peeled potatoes. Even so, many of them got frostbitten feet. In some cases, this meant that they had to have their feet removed.

Although cold and hunger took its toll, the men were most apt to die from sickness. Two-thirds of the 2,000 men who died that winter did so from the flu, typhus, and typhoid. In fact, for each man in the Continental Army who died in battle, another ten died from disease! Although the men did not starve, food was scarce. To add to the Army's problems, area storeowners would rather sell supplies for British money than the near-worthless Continental currency.

But the Continental Army managed to rise above these hardships. The men drilled and became organized troops. Cannons were fixed, and the men trained in their use. The Army left the Valley Forge encampment on June 19, 1778. Just nine days later, Washington's troops showed their competence. They beat the British in the Battle of Monmouth in New Jersey.

*South Carolina and Georgia did not have troops at Valley Forge.

The Continental Army's Winter at Valley Forge

The American Revolution
British vs. Colonists

British

Disadvantages	Advantages
–	**+**

- soldiers unfamiliar with the land
- difficulty in getting supplies from overseas
- many British citizens were against the war

- large, well-trained troops—at that time considered the best army in the world
- had paid German troops (Hessians)
- experienced military leaders
- strong navy
- factories to make war supplies
- funds to wage war

Colonists

Disadvantages	Advantages
–	**+**

- small, untrained army
- inexperienced military leaders
- no navy
- few factories to make war supplies
- few funds to wage war
- many colonists sympathized with the British

- soldiers familiar with the land
- troops fighting for their own liberty
- after October 1777, received French military aid and money

The Continental Army's Winter at Valley Forge

1. The Continental Army gathered at Valley Forge, Pennsylvania on

    a. July 4, 1776.   c. December 19, 1777.

    b. September 27, 1777.   d. June 19, 1778.

2. Which of the 13 colonies did not have any troops at Valley Forge?

    a. North Carolina   c. Connecticut

    b. South Carolina   d. Massachusetts

3. The troops at Valley Forge did not spend six months learning how to

    a. build log cabins.   c. fire cannons.

    b. aim guns.   d. march in formation.

4. During the American Revolution, sickness claimed more soldiers' lives than battles did. True or False? Explain.

_____

_____

_____

5. Why did Great Britain feel confident that it could win the war? Use details from the graphic organizer.

_____

_____

_____

_____

_____

6. Which disadvantage was the worst for the British? Which one was the worst for the American colonists? Defend your stance.

_____

_____

_____

_____

_____

The Lewis and Clark Expedition

President Thomas Jefferson bought the Louisiana Territory in April 1803. He hoped that the land had a waterway that went from the Mississippi River to the Pacific Ocean. Jefferson hired Meriwether Lewis to explore and make a map of the new land. Lewis asked his friend, William Clark, to help him lead the expedition.

In the winter of 1803, the pair hired 40 men and set up camp near St. Louis, Missouri. During the cold months, the men built boats and practiced shooting. The trip's leaders bought gifts of beads, pipes, belts, and knives for Native American chiefs.

On May 14, 1804, the group set out in three keelboats. Lewis and Clark thought that the round trip would take about 18 months. Instead it took more than two years. During that time the leaders kept logbooks. They drew pictures and made notes about plants and animals that they had never seen before.

Traveling by boat was hard. Rocks lurked below the surface of the water, ready to damage a boat that sailed into them. Where the water was too low, the boats had to be pulled or carried by the men. Thousands of mosquitoes attacked the men, and bears chased them. At last they reached the Great Plains. There they shot and ate buffalo.

Then the group met a Sioux tribe whose chief didn't like his gifts. He tried to take one of their boats. In response the men aimed their guns at the Sioux braves. They turned and left. Lewis, Clark, and their weary group were glad to meet the friendly Mandan tribe. They spent the winter with them.

In April 1805, they headed west again with three new members. A French trapper, his Native American wife, Sacagawea, and their baby boy came along. Sacagawea was quite helpful. She knew which plants they could eat and use for medicine. She saved things when a boat flipped. When the expedition needed horses in order to cross the Rocky Mountains, she got them from a tribe whose leader she knew.

Danger was a constant companion. One man was blind in one eye and had limited sight in the other. He accidentally shot Lewis! The group almost starved going across the Rocky Mountains. Yet just one man died on the trip, and it was from sickness.

The expedition returned home on September 23, 1806. The men had covered 7,700 miles by boat, horse, and on foot in one of the biggest adventures of all time.

The Lewis and Clark Expedition

Congress gave Meriwether Lewis $2,500 to buy supplies for the expedition. As he spent the money, Lewis made this list for Congress.

In addition to the money from Congress, President Jefferson gave Lewis a letter of credit. The letter meant that storeowners could give Lewis things and then write to the U.S. government to get payment. Although Lewis spent money wisely, he ran up a bill of $39,000. That was a huge sum back then.

Mathematical instruments	$217
Arms and clothing	$81
Equipment for camp0 (tents, pots and pans, etc)	$255
Medicine and bandages	$55
Means of transportation (boats, horses)	$430
Gifts for Indians	$696
Provisions(flour, salt, beans, etc)	$224
Materials to make portable packs (like backpacks)	$55
Wages of hunters, guides, and interpreters*	$300
Money for expenses to move the group from Nashville, TN to the last white settlement in Missouri	$87
Cash for incidentals (odds and ends)	$87
Total	$2,500

*people who could speak with the Native American tribes

The Lewis and Clark Expedition

1. Lewis and Clark left St. Louis, Missouri, in

    a. April 1803.   c. April 1805.

    b. May 1804.   d. September 1806.

2. Who turned out to be a surprisingly important member of the expedition?

    a. a woman from the Mandan tribe   c. a French trapper

    b. the man who accidentally shot Lewis   d. a Sioux chief

3. Which would not have been a gift the group would give to a Native American chief?

    a. glass beads   c. a sharp knife

    b. a leather belt   d. a keelboat

4. The Lewis and Clark expedition cost the U. S. government more than $41,000. True or False? Explain your answer.

_____

_____

_____

5. What were the two most expensive items on the list that Lewis gave to the government? Name the items and what was spent.

_____

_____

_____

_____

_____

6. Did Lewis spend enough money on food to take on the trip? Defend your stance.

_____

_____

_____

_____

_____

Explosion on the *U.S.S. Maine*

By 1500, the island of Cuba was under Spanish control. In 1868, the natives rebelled against Spain's leadership. The government had many people killed. The freedom fighters continued to rebel. But they had little success. In 1895, the Cubans tried a new tactic. They sent fiction disguised as news to American newspapers. The papers' editors did not check the facts. They just published the stories. Some were shocking lies. One article stated that the Spaniards had killed one quarter of all the Cubans and then eaten them!

Americans read these stories. They grumbled about how U.S. President McKinley wasn't helping the Cubans. So in September 1897, McKinley told the Spanish government to stop persecuting the Cubans. He also sent the *U.S.S. Maine* to Havana, Cuba. It was the first modern U.S. battleship. Longer than a football field, it took nearly nine years to build. The ship arrived on January 25, 1898. Its captain got a note from some Spaniards. It warned that the *Maine* would sink. He put the ship on alert. Even so, on February 15 at 9:30 P.M. the *Maine* blew up. The captain and most officers lived. They were in their quarters. But 262 sailors were not as lucky.

Some of the officers thought that the Spanish had hit the ship with a torpedo or a floating mine. Others said that Cubans did it. They wanted to start a war that they hoped would give them their freedom. Two survivors said that they had heard a cannon blast. Both American and Spanish experts studied the wreck. The Americans said that the ship had touched a mine. The Spanish said that one of the ship's boilers had blown up.

Although the real cause of the explosion was unclear, Americans were angry. On April 25, 1898, Congress declared war on Spain. The fighting lasted just 109 days. Spain gave up. A peace treaty was signed in December. It gave Cuba its freedom. America paid Spain $20 million for Guam, Puerto Rico, and the Philippines.

But the questions about the *Maine* remain. Did the Spanish cause the explosion to make the Americans leave Cuba? Did Cuban rebels wreck the ship because they felt the Americans would get rid of the Spanish? Or did the ship's coal bunkers overheat? Other ships built at that time had that trouble. If a bunker overheated, it could cause an explosion. Yet the *Maine* had an alarm to let the sailors know if the bunkers' temperature was too warm. It never sounded.

American William Randolph Hearst owned a newspaper. Newspapers sell best during wars. A photographer stated that Hearst sent him to Cuba to cover the war before it began. When the man protested, Hearst told him, "You furnish* the pictures. I'll furnish the war." Could Hearst have had a bomb planted on the ship? No one knows for sure.

*provide

Explosion on the *U.S.S. Maine*

This is a condensed version of a letter written by Lieutenant George Preston Blow the morning after the explosion.

On Board: S. S. City of Washington

February 16, 1898

Dearest,

I sent you two cablegrams last night telling you of my safety, and hoping they both reached you before the morning papers, and that you were spared the agony of suspense and uncertainty.

I cannot tell you now of my miraculous escape, as the scene is still too terrible to recall, even had I the time. I was in my room when the ship blew up, and when I rushed for the ladder leading on deck I found the door closed. In pitch darkness, with explosion following explosion and expecting each second to be blown into the air, or drowned by the inrushing water, I found the other door and reached the ladder.

The whole ship was blown into the air, except the officers' quarters—which explain why so many of them were saved. In fact we only lost two, and only a few were slightly wounded. Among the men, we saved about 50, leaving about 250 dead. I cannot write of the horrors now. Each man lived a lifetime of horror in a few seconds and all would like to forget it if possible.

I escaped in my trousers, undershirt, and socks. Of course I lost my glasses and haven't a cent in the world. The Captain will look out for us when he gets time. At present we have other and sadder duties to our lost shipmates.

In my struggle in the darkness and water, you and the babies were in my mind, dearest. I found time to help one poor devil to climb to a place of safety. Whether he escaped or who he was I do not know. Nearly all the saved among the crew were people who had blown overboard and afterwards picked up. One man was picked up a hundred yards away.

Whether we were torpedoed by the Spanish, blown up by a mine, or whether the Cubans did it to bring on a war—or whether it was one of these spontaneous explosions, we do not know. I hate to suspect the Spanish, and their actions, sympathy, and assistance seems to indicate that they are ignorant of the cause. For the present we must withhold our judgment. It is almost certain that Congress will declare war today, without waiting—and it is possible that we may be prisoners before night. If so, you must not worry, as we are sure to receive good treatment on account of the sympathy of the people.

Love and kisses for the dear little ones and a heart full to bursting of love and longing for you my darling. I must go to work.

Love to all,

Preston

The Spanish American War Centennial Website. "Letter 1, Written the Day After the Maine Went Down." **http://www.spanamwar.com/blowlet1.htm**

Explosion on the *U.S.S. Maine*

1. How many people died when the *U.S.S. Maine* blew up?

   a. 50 men   c. 250 men

   b. 109 men   d. 262 men

2. After how many years of rebellion did the Cubans receive their freedom?

   a. 10 years   c. 30 years

   b. 20 years   d. 40 years

3. Since the Americans were sympathetic to their cause, why did anyone suspect that Cuban rebels might have wrecked the *U.S.S. Maine*?

   a. The Cubans did not really believe that Americans were sympathetic to their cause.

   b. The Cubans hoped that the wreck would cause a war between Spain and America that America would win.

   c. The Cubans thought that the *U.S.S. Maine* was really a Spanish ship.

   d. The Cubans felt that the Americans were trying to take over Cuba by having a ship in Havana's harbor.

4. At the end of the Spanish-American War, Spain gave the United States Puerto Rico, the Philippines, and Guam. True or False? Explain your answer.

   _____

   _____

   _____

5. Did Lt. George Preston Blow believe that the Spanish deliberately damaged the *U.S.S. Maine* or would kill its officers if war was declared? Quote his letter in your response.

   _____

   _____

   _____

   _____

   _____

6. Which theory do you believe explains what happened to the *U.S.S. Maine*? Defend your stance.

   _____

   _____

   _____

   _____

   _____

Assassinated!

Civil War veteran William McKinley was elected as the 25th U.S. president in 1896. Four years later he began a second term. During his time in office, he set the United States on a path toward world leadership. He led the nation as it came out of an economic depression and won the Spanish-American War of 1898. The war's treaty gave America control of Guam, the Philippines, and Puerto Rico. Holding more land increased America's power in the eyes of the world.

Just months into his second term, McKinley gave a speech on September 5, 1901. It was in Buffalo, New York. He wanted to lower the U.S. tariffs (taxes) on goods coming into the country. And he wanted other nations to reduce their tariffs on goods coming from America. He said that free trade would help the United States to grow richer.

Not everyone agreed with him. One such man, Leon Czolgosz, was in the crowd. This man was an anarchist. Such a person is against all forms of government. The day after the president spoke, Czolgosz went to a party. It was at the Temple of Music. He carried a gun. It was covered with a handkerchief wrapped around his hand like a bandage. When the president reached out his hand to shake Czolgosz's, the man fired the gun. The bullet went right into the president's stomach. The crowd grabbed the assassin. McKinley said, "Don't let them hurt him." Then he was rushed to the hospital. The president survived the surgery that removed the bullet. But his wound became infected. On September 14, McKinley died. He was the third president murdered in office.

Vice President Theodore Roosevelt was a hero of the Spanish-American War. He was also in New York state. His aides found him hiking in the Adirondack Mountains. He rushed to Buffalo. But the president had already died. Roosevelt was sworn into office that same day.

Czolgosz was caught and found guilty. He was executed in an electric chair in October. To honor the president, a mountain in Alaska was named Mount McKinley. It is the highest peak in North America.

Assassinated!

Courtesy of the Library of Congress, "Leslie's Weekly McKinley," LC-USZ62-96528

Assassinated!

1. President William McKinley was a veteran of the

   a. Revolutionary War.

   b. War of 1812.

   c. Civil War.

   d. Spanish-American War.

2. President McKinley's vice president was

   a. Leon Czolgosz.

   b. Theodore Roosevelt.

   c. Franklin D. Roosevelt.

   d. not mentioned in the article.

3. Tariffs are

   a. taxes on foreign goods coming into the country.

   b. property taxes.

   c. a type of income tax.

   d. taxes on goods made in one's own nation.

4. President McKinley died eight days after he was shot. True or False? Explain your answer.

_____

_____

_____

5. How would the *Leslie's Weekly* magazine cover help or hurt the new president's public support?

_____

_____

_____

_____

6. Would President McKinley have approved of his assassin's execution? Defend your stance.

_____

_____

_____

_____

_____

The Justice Bell

Have you ever seen the Liberty Bell? You can stand in line for hours to get a glimpse of it. It has its own pavilion in Philadelphia, Pennsylvania. Or you could go to the George Washington Memorial Chapel. It's in Valley Forge, Pennsylvania. You can walk right up and touch a close replica of the Liberty Bell there. It hangs in the foyer of the church. The bell is missing the famous crack, however. It was cast years later when bell makers knew how to make stronger bells.

Another difference is the inscription. The Liberty Bell states: "Proclaim liberty throughout the land unto all the inhabitants thereof." This one states: "Establish justice throughout the land unto all the inhabitants thereof." Why? This bell is the Justice Bell. Unlike the Liberty Bell, it can still ring. But it didn't ring for the first time until five years after it was made! This bell was a symbol of the woman's suffrage movement. Having women vote was a matter of justice. So the bell did not ring until women had won that right.

The Justice Bell was cast in 1915. It cost $2,000. A rich woman paid for it. But its tour costs were funded with nickels and dimes. Women's rights supporters gave the money. The bell toured Pennsylvania from June until November. It traveled in a special truck made to carry its bulk. It weighed a ton! During that time the bell visited all of the state's 67 counties. Parades, bands, and banners greeted it. Women stood on the truck next to the bell. They gave speeches. They said that women were as much American citizens as men. They deserved the right to vote. At each rally, the women chanted, "Father, brother, husband, son, vote for Amendment Number One." It was up to male voters to pass the state's amendment for women's suffrage.

The amendment failed. But the women did not give up. They just changed their strategy. They turned away from trying to get state amendments. They decided to go for a Constitutional amendment. They were determined to win the right to vote for women throughout the nation. So the Justice Bell went to rallies in Washington, D.C. and Chicago, Illinois.

In 1920 the Nineteenth Amendment to the Constitution gave all women in America the right to vote. One month after the Amendment was ratified, the Justice Bell rang for the first time.

The Justice Bell

American soldiers joined World War I in Europe in April 1917. This ad was published in the *New York Post* that year:

Would the soldier give her the ballot?

Courtesy of the Library of Congress, "Would the soldier give her the ballot?" LC- USZ62-124332

The Justice Bell

1. The inscription on the Liberty Bell and the Justice Bell differs by

   a. one word.

   b. two words.

   c. three words.

   d. four words.

2. Why was a Constitutional amendment for woman's suffrage better than state amendments for woman's suffrage?

   a. because it passed faster

   b. because it could be ratified with fewer votes

   c. because it gave American women and women in foreign nations the right to vote

   d. because it gave all American women the right to vote instead of having to win the same battle in every state

3. When a bell is cast, it is

   a. rung.

   b. made.

   c. put into a steeple.

   d. thrown away.

4. The Pennsylvania state amendment to give women the right to vote did not pass. True or False? Explain.

   _____

   _____

   _____

5. What is the answer to the question posed in the *New York Post* ad? How do you know?

   _____

   _____

   _____

   _____

6. Would you prefer to see the Liberty Bell or the Justice Bell? Why?

   _____

   _____

   _____

   _____

The Japanese-American Internment Camps of World War II

The Japanese bombed Pearl Harbor on December 7, 1941. They ruined most of the United States' Pacific fleet of ships and planes. The next day, America declared war on Japan.

People immediately viewed Japanese-Americans with suspicion. They thought that they were spies for Japan. This was true even for those who had been born in America and were clearly patriotic! Within a few weeks, Japanese-American men were rounded up and put in jail. Their families had to give any radios, cameras, binoculars, and guns to the police. Their bank accounts were frozen. They could not get their own money from the bank. They could only go out in public in daylight. And they could not go more than five miles from home.

On February 20, 1942, more than 110,000 people of Japanese descent left their homes. About 70,000 of these people were U.S. citizens. They could bring only what they could carry in their arms. They went to fairgrounds and racetracks enclosed by barbed wire fences. Armed guards stood watch.

Each family had a small "room," no matter how many members it had. Most of these rooms had been horse stalls. Army cots were the only furniture. There was no running water or heat. About 300 people shared the toilets and showers. They waited in long lines for meals. The Japanese-Americans spent the spring and summer of 1942 in these makeshift quarters. Then they moved to one of 10 camps. The camps were in Idaho, California, Wyoming, Arizona, or Arkansas. They had rows of ugly barracks covered with black tar paper. Each room had a closet, a window, and a light bulb hanging from the ceiling. Rooms were one of three sizes. If you had a big family, you got a larger room.

The people made the best of a bad situation. They planted gardens for food. Students went to schools inside the camps. But they had no books or paper. Despite their lack of freedom, about 800 young Japanese-American men from the camps volunteered to fight. They served in the U.S. armed forces in Europe.

The Japanese-Americans lived in the barracks until the war ended in 1946. Then they were set free. But they had to start their lives over. They had to find jobs. And their homes were not given back to them! Congress passed a law in 1948. It gave up to $2,500 to individual Japanese-Americans for their losses. Forty years later all surviving Japanese-Americans who had lived in the camps got $20,000.

The Japanese-American Internment Camps of World War II

Courtesy of the Library of Congress, "I am an American," LC-USZ62-23602

This is a store window at the corner of 13th and Franklin streets in San Francisco, California. Its Japanese American owner posted the sign in March 1942, just days after Executive Order 9066 announced the forced relocation of Japanese American citizens.

The sign did no good. The storeowner was sent to a War Relocation center for the duration of World War II.

The Japanese-American Internment Camps of World War II

1. There were no Japanese-American relocation camps in the state of

   a. Arkansas.   c. California.

   b. Wyoming.   d. New Mexico.

2. Surviving Japanese-American internees received $20,000 from the U.S. government in

   a. 1942.   c. 1948.

   b. 1946.   d. 1988.

3. Living in an internment camp was most like living in a

   a. prison.   c. summer camp.

   b. boarding school.   d. Nazi concentration camp.

4. Most of the Japanese-Americans moved to relocation centers were U.S. citizens. True or False? Explain.

_____

_____

_____

5. Look at the photo. Why did the storeowner place the sign in his shop window?

_____

_____

_____

_____

6. If you had been a young Japanese-American male living in an internment camp, would you have volunteered to fight in the U.S. armed forces? Why or why not?

_____

_____

_____

_____

_____

Answer Key

page 12

1. a   2. b   3. c

4. True. She died in Auburn, New York, where she operated a home for poor, ill, and homeless blacks.

5. The reason $10,000 was offered was Harriet's capture was to encourage everyone to want to catch her. The plantation owners wanted her caught because she was so good at getting slaves out of the South. For every slave that escaped, the plantation owner lost money (the value of the slave).

6. Yes, Harriet did the right thing by threatening to kill the runaways who wanted to turn back because if they were tortured, they might give away information about the Underground Railroad. Then the escape route would be ruined for others. Also, the people who helped slaves on the Underground Railroad were risking their own lives. If a runaway gave information on these people, they could be killed or their homes burned by angry plantation owners. OR No, Harriet did not do the right thing by threatening to kill the runaways who wanted to turn back because it is wrong to threaten violence. Harriet could have explained why they couldn't turn back and used encouragement to make the slaves go on.

page 15

1. b   2. d   3. c

4. True. Nellie felt that the care of the insane should be improved. She gives details in her articles and in her testimony to the jury about how bad the conditions were in the Women's Lunatic Asylum. She wrote that the treatment of the women was so bad that it would drive anyone insane. She told of beatings, chokings, starvation, near-drownings, and a complete lack of compassion for the patients. (Responses must include some of the abuses Nellie found in the asylum.)

5. The jury believed Nellie because she included so many details in her newspaper articles about her experiences there that it was clear that she had really lived there. It would be hard for a person to make up such realistic details about things that hadn't occurred. Also, the jury knew that Nellie had no reason to lie. Why would she try to bring about reforms if none were needed?

6. I think that Urena's story was more upsetting because the nurses made her cry on purpose and then hit her when she wouldn't stop crying! Then they choked her and locked her in a closet! No one should treat an animal the way they treated that poor woman. OR I think that Louise Schanz's story was more upsetting because Louise probably wasn't even insane and yet she was committed for life to a terrible place just because she didn't know the language!

page 18

1. b   2. c   3. b

4. False. Anthony was an agent for the American Anti-Slavery Society and wanted blacks as well as women to be educated.

5. Anthony's main goals for women were the right to vote, to own property, and to get an education. She first showed interest in women's issues in 1852 and died in 1906, so she worked for women's rights for 54 years.

6. Yes, Anthony would have been more successful if she had focused solely on women's suffrage because then she could have spent all her time on one issue. She spent many years working to free slaves and never met with a U.S. president until the year before she died. If she had put all her efforts into women's suffrage, she might have lived to see the amendment passed that gave them the vote. OR No, Anthony would not have been more successful if she had focused solely on women's suffrage because she wanted to help women and blacks in general. She wanted social reform for both groups. She succeeded in showing Americans that both groups had much to contribute to society if they were allowed to do so.

page 21

1. c   2. d   3. b

4. False. Sand filtration of drinking water began in 1890 and is still used today.

5. Chlorine was first added to the drinking water in Philadelphia in 1908. It was soon obvious that it helped to curb typhoid fever. The number of typhoid cases had dropped the year before (1907). However, the number of cases of typhoid had gone up and down for many years prior to that. From the time chlorination was added, the number of typhoid cases never rose again.

6. Yes, the people in charge of water utilities nationwide were wrong not to adopt Wolman's chlorination as soon as he made it known. He had shown that it was safe and effective. During the years in which the water utilities resisted chlorination, many Americans died of diseases like typhoid fever. OR No, the people in charge of water utilities nationwide were not wrong in waiting to adopt Wolman's chlorination. The heads of the utilities knew that chlorine is a poison. They took a wait-and-see approach because they had a hard time believing it was good to add a poison to drinking water. They were not wrong to want several years of proof that showed the chlorine wasn't going to hurt anyone.

page 24

1. d   2. a   3. b

4. False. Along with Sugihara, his whole family was imprisoned in Romania for 18 months (a year and a half). This happened because he disobeyed the Japanese government to help the Jews.

5. Marta Goldstein is writing to thank Sugihara for giving her and her children the visas they needed to leave

Answer Key (Cont.)

Lithuania. She says that her husband died in Auschwitz/a concentration camp/a death camp. Her son and daughter are alive and living with her. Because she has both of her children, she feels that she has much more than many Jews do. Many Jews lost some or all of their children in the Holocaust.

6. Yes, the Japanese government did the right thing by firing Sugihara because he had defied its orders. No employer will keep an employee who does something after he or she was told three times not to do it. OR No, the Japanese government did not do the right thing by firing Sugihara because what he did was morally right, even though he did defy orders. The government should have recognized that he was a brave, decent man and kept him as an employee.

page 27

1. b   2. c   3. d

4. False. Mandela was imprisoned because he spoke out against apartheid. He was put in jail for 27 years because he disagreed with the government's leaders.

5. Mandela gives credit to the millions of people around the world, the governments, and the organizations that pressured the South African leadership to end apartheid. He said that if the world had not stood up to the South African leaders, they would have continued apartheid.

6. Yes, Mandela should have put the former South African apartheid leaders into prison because they had committed a crime against humanity. OR No, Mandela should not have put the former South African apartheid leaders into prison because then he would have made them into political prisoners because they disagreed with him. That's what was done to him. He didn't want to mistreat them as they had mistreated him.

page 30

1. b   2. d   3. a

4. False. According to the zoo's advertisement, the most venomous animal in the world is the sea wasp. OR False. According to the zoo's advertisement, the most venomous snake/reptile in the world is the striped sea snake.

5. The Cedarhurst Zoo must make sure that visitors cannot touch the animals in the Toxic Terror exhibit. The animals must be kept behind glass (people could put their fingers through cage bars) and access must be locked.

6. Students must select one of these six creatures: poison dart frogs, stingrays, scorpions, tarantulas, wandering spiders, or striped sea snakes. They must give a reason for choosing it as the most frightening, such as: "I think stingrays are the scariest because they are the ones I am most apt to encounter. My sister was stung by a ray and threw up for hours; it was a stingray that killed the Crocodile Hunter, etc."

page 33

1. c   2. a   3. d

4. True. These people had endured the Holocaust, and the camps held horrible memories for the Jewish refugees. OR False. The refugees were not mistreated there and they had nowhere else to go until Israel was officially created.

5. The note's author wants the British soldiers and officers to feel guilty/ashamed for bringing the Jews back to Germany—the very place they had just escaped from. The writer speaks of being taken back to the "murder people" who killed parents and children. The writer accuses the troops of "sending us back to pains, sufferings, and downfall!" The writer also states that they are "waging a battle against peaceful innocent people."

6. Yes, the British did the right thing by interfering with the *Exodus 1947* because they knew that the creation of Israel would create great turmoil in the Middle East. They were trying to prevent that from happening and were simply enforcing a 1923 decree by the League of Nations. OR No, the British should not have interfered with the Exodus 1947 because the peace treaty that ended World War II had set up a homeland for the Jews. The British should have respected the peace treaty. Also, attacking an unarmed ship was a brutal thing to do and caused the death of three people and injured 30.

page 36

1. d   2. c   3. a

4. True. The colonists started out on the wrong foot by killing members of an innocent tribe after one of their men was killed. Before that the Croatoans had been friendly, and Manteo had even joined their group. OR False. The colonists started out on the right foot with the Native Americans because Manteo immediately joined their group, and the Croatoans were described as friendly. Later they may have ruined their relationship with the Croatoans after killing members of their tribe in error.

5. The historians say that the colonists were heavily armed, and their guns could kill and wound from a farther (safer) distance than the Native Americans' weapons. Also, if the colonists were taken by surprise or fighting for their lives, no one would have had the time to carve CRO.

6. I think that the colonists set sail for England and were shipwrecked because there was a bad drought and the people wanted to go home. A few men could've built a second boat so there'd be enough room to carry them all. They probably would've set sail in the summer, when that area has hurricanes that could shipwreck them. OR I think that the colonists were killed during a Native American attack because they had problems with the Roanokes killing a man almost immediately. Then they made enemies of the Croatoans by killing

them accidentally. The fort is evidence that they were trying to protect themselves. The Native Americans may have been picking them off a few at a time, which gave them time to carve the word. OR I think that the colonists were killed by a hurricane and a few survivors merged with the Croatoan tribe. This area is known for hurricanes, a kind of storm with which the colonists were unfamiliar. A storm surge could've wiped out most of them, and the few survivors had to join the a Native American tribe to stay alive. OR I think that the colonists merged with the Croatoan tribe, maybe because they were starving from a drought. This is the Lumbees' oral tradition, and there's no reason for them to lie. Also, their blue eyes and light skin show that these Native Americans had white ancestors. OR I think that the colonists split into two groups. Chief Powhatan said that he wiped out one of these groups. He had no reason to lie, and he gave a valid reason for why he killed them.

page 39

1. a   2. b   3. d

4. False. People are most likely to recycle when they have curbside pickup because that is more convenient than having to take things to a recycling center.

5. The "other" category includes such things as appliances, toys, computers, sports equipment, TVs, stereos, furniture, mattresses, and construction waste (shingles, concrete, etc.). (Give credit for any three responses—as long as they aren't an item from the named categories of the pie chart such as tires or clothing.)

6. Yes, recycling should be required with a big fine for anyone who fails to do it because we are running out of landfill space and wasting resources by dumping recyclable things into landfills. The fine would make people take the requirement seriously and help to fund programs to teach people the importance of recycling. Based on the pie graph, 59 percent of all trash is recyclable. (plastic + metal + paper + glass) OR No, recycling shouldn't be required because it would be too hard to enforce. Who could keep track of who wasn't recycling in order to charge a fine? It would be more effective to teach people the importance of recycling or show them how recycling will benefit them (lower taxes or prices, etc.).

page 42

1. c   2. a   3. d

4. False. Asian carp were imported to clean up algae in ponds in Arkansas. OR False. Floods swept Asian carp into the Illinois River.

5. Alien fish have the highest number of species and alien mammals have the lowest number of species in the United States.

6. Yes, alien species should be killed using whatever means is necessary because they damage the environment and wipe out native species. The only way to stop such things from happening is to kill the alien species. OR No, alien species should not be killed because that's cruelty to animals. It's not the animal's fault-- it's some human's fault that it is in the new environment causing trouble. The alien animals should be caught and returned to their native lands. Or they can be fed birth control to keep them from reproducing, so they will slowly die out in the new environment.

page 45

1. d   2. b   3. c

4. False. The men called it hardship duty and needed bonuses to encourage them to work on these ships. They hated the tropical diseases and the cruelty they saw on the slave ships.

5. The date on the slave auction poster is 1835, 20 years after the anti-slave trade laws started being enforced. This auction took place because the anti-slave trade laws were meant to prevent new slaves from entering America. The laws did nothing to help the slaves who were already here or those that were born into slavery.

6. The slave auction poster states that husbands, wives, and children are for sale. It doesn't say that the same person must buy the family. The worst part of slavery was the fact that it split up families. That was incredibly cruel. OR The slave auction poster brags about how hardworking, intelligent, competent each slave is in order to get people to him/her. The worst part of slavery was that these people were bought and sold like animals even though their "owner" openly acknowledges all their human traits. (Accept any reasonable, supported answer.)

page 48

1. b   2. c   3. d

4. True. The U.S. Mint in Denver started making coins in 1906, so 2106 is 200 years later.

5. The U.S. Mint in Denver holds a world record for striking/making/minting more than 15 billion circulating coins in one year.

6. Yes, the Congressional Medal of Honor should be given only to U.S. citizens. Since the U.S. government gives the award, it should be used to honor its own citizens. There are plenty of Americans who deserve the medal for what they do to help others. Foreigners should be honored by their own governments. OR No, the Congressional Medal of Honor shouldn't be given only to U.S. citizens because the purpose is to honor those people who do things to help others. There are many deserving people that are not Americans.

Answer Key *(Cont.)*

page 51

1. b 2. c 3. a

4. False. No one knows how the pyramids were built. Some people think that levers were used and others claim spiral ramps or wet tafla ramps were used. OR True. Some people believe that levers were used to build the pyramids, but not everyone agrees. (Allow either answer, as long as the student acknowledges that there are other theories, and that none is a certainty.)

5. The granite plugs were put in place after the king was buried to keep out grave robbers. The only other route to the king's chamber was to go underground and then back up through the workers' descending and service corridors. Perhaps the pyramid designers thought that the thieves would give up if they had to go to great lengths to reach the riches. Yet, in spite of the granite plugs, the thieves removed all the riches and the mummy.

6. Yes, the pyramids should be open to the public. The ancient Egyptian mummies are in museums now, so they are no longer resting inside the tombs. Letting the public go into the pyramids is educational and shows people how advanced the ancient Egyptian civilization really was. OR No, the pyramids should not be open to the public. Other kinds of tombs are not open to the public, so pyramids should not be. Also, people are hard on structures and may wreck the pyramids by taking little pieces from them as souvenirs.

page 54

1. b 2. a 3. c

4. True. The tourism money it brings in is so valuable that the Chinese government spent money to repair the most popular parts of the Great Wall.

5. No, the Great Wall did not prevent trade caravans from traveling across China. The photograph shows that there were gates in the Great Wall for this purpose. The caravan probably had to let soldiers guarding the Wall know that they needed to come through. If the soldiers thought that they were really traders (and not the disguised enemies), the gates would be opened just long enough for them to move through.

6. Yes, it was good that the Great Wall isolated China from Europe. The Chinese obviously had problems with Europeans and Asians invading their nation. Whenever a nation is invaded, people are killed, injured, or enslaved. Isolation was a small price to pay in order to prevent invasions. OR No, it was not good that the Great Wall isolated China from Europe because ideas and inventions created in one place did not spread to the other. It limited the knowledge of one area from the other. Now that knowledge is shared among most nations, technology, medicine, and inventions improve fast. (Accept any reasonable responses.)

page 57

1. d 2. a 3. b

4. False. Roggeveen lived nearly 200 years before Heyerdahl stated his theory. And Roggeveen did not say how he thought Easter Island was populated. He just reported what the people looked like.

5. Some archaeologists say that Heyerdahl tampered with evidence to make it fit his theory. They also discounted his raft trip across the ocean because he was towed 50 miles out to sea to avoid the currents that would have trapped Tiki's raft near the South American shore.

6. I believe that that the Rapa Nui came from other Polynesian islands. They look like other Polynesians, and there is no real evidence that people from Peru ever visited Easter Island. OR I believe that Easter Island was settled by people from Polynesia and people from Peru due to the similarities between the two groups, including spearheads, sweet potatoes, and the story of Kon-Tiki. OR I believe that the adult children of Basque sailors and Polynesian women settled Easter Island because the Rapa Nui have Basque genes. There's no other way that they could have those genes. Also, this theory is supported by Roggeveen's reports of dark- and light-skinned people.

page 60

1. c 2. d 3. b

4. True. You can tell that Shah Jahan and Mumtaz Mahal were Muslims because there are verses from the Koran written on the main gate and tomb walls. Near the tomb there is a mosque and four minarets. Muslims use these structures for worship.

5. Muslims cannot make images of people, so no paintings or sculptures exist to show us what the couple looked like. Like most Islamic art, the Taj Mahal has geometric and floral patterns.

6. Yes, I would love to visit the Taj Mahal. I'd like to go to India and see this grand tomb for myself. I bet it would be unforgettable. OR No, I wouldn't like to visit the Taj Mahal. I don't really care about beautiful buildings. I don't like to fly, which is what I'd have to do to get to India, etc. (Allow reasonable responses.)

page 63

1. c 2. c 3. a

4. False. The Panama Canal passes through Gatun Lake and Miraflores Lake. OR False. The Panama Canal has three sets of locks, not lakes.

5. The Gatun, Pedro Miguel, and Miraflores Locks in the Panama Canal were built in pairs to let ships move through in both directions at the same time.

6. Yes, the Panama Canal should continue to charge tolls because the money can be used to maintain and repair the Canal, pay the workers who operate it, and buy new

equipment (like the locomotives) when things break. OR No, the Panama Canal should not continue to charge tolls because ships must use the Canal. Charging tolls increases the cost of the things carried on the ships.

page 66

1. a 2. d 3. b

4. True. The diagram shows that the water level in the lake is higher than the Yangtze River below the dam. Also the water intake pipe is angled downward so that water flows downhill (from gravity) to turn the turbines. The turbine's spinning makes electricity.

5. There is a grate over the water intake so that debris (logs, branches, trash) in the water doesn't get into the turbines and wreck or clog them.

6. Yes, the Three Gorges Dam should have been built because it helps to control the deadly flooding of the Yangtze River. It also generates clean electrical power for a nation that needs more electricity. OR No, the Three Gorges Dam shouldn't have been built because it flooded 1.2 million people's homes and farms, ruined forests, drowned animals, and left important historical sites underwater.

page 69

1. b 2. b 3. c

4. True. All of the plants died and drinking water was contaminated. Almost 12,000 died in the eruption but another 80,000 died later due to hunger, disease, and lack of clean drinking water.

5. In terms of deadly volcanoes, the worst nation in which to live is Indonesia. Four eruptions appear on the chart which shows that the number of people killed by volcanoes in Indonesia is more than 137,000! Mount Tambora is in Indonesia.

6. Yes. The volcano could erupt again and if it does, it will kill people and destroy many homes. OR No. Although the people would still lose their property, today the volcano is monitored so adequate warning could be given for the people to evacuate. Now there are rescue organizations that would help after the disaster, too.

page 72

1. a 2. d 3. c

4. True. Religious issues made the disaster even worse. There had been religious tension between the two islands for hundreds of years. Most of the British Protestant landlords did not care about the suffering of their Irish Catholic tenants. While the Irish people stood there starving, the landlords exported the food from Ireland to England and Scotland!

5. The magazine cover is trying to bring the desperate situation in Ireland to the attention of the people in America. The Irish woman's family is huddled behind her as she stands hailing an American ship. She is

waving a white hanky like an SOS for help. It is clear that she is hoping that Americans will send food to feed her and her family.

6. Since the *Harper's Weekly* magazine cover is dated February 25, 1880, and it is appealing to the Americans for help, it looks like the British did not quickly step in to help the Irish during this second famine. Also, the British prime minister apologized for the nation's lack of action in 1997. OR Since the first famine lasted for six years and the second one lasted for two, it seems likely that the British did step in to help more quickly during the second disaster. The Americans helped, too, as evidenced by the magazine cover, so the second famine was not as severe as the first.

page 75

1. a 2. d 3. b

4. True. The people of Johnstown had some warning of the possibility of a flood disaster because the Stony Creek dam broke earlier the same day and the people saw debris floating down the river. A telegram was sent to Johnstown about one hour before the South Fork dam burst. OR False. Most of the people of Johnstown did not know about the Stony Creek dam breaking—only those who saw the debris floating down the river. Also, in 1889, there was no way to spread the word rapidly after the telegram was received. So the majority of Johnstown citizens never knew about the telegram's warning until after the disaster.

5. Disinfectants are needed to clean things. After the flood, everything was dirty—coated in oil, dirt, sewage, etc. Under these conditions, disease can spread fast. The disinfectants were used to make things safe for people to touch and use.

6. Yes, the president of the South Fork Hunting and Fishing Club admitted that the dam caused the disaster, so the Club should have given money to pay for the clean up of the city. Also, the dam had not been well-maintained. The Club knew that thousands of people lived downstream and would suffer if the dam broke, yet had done little to prevent the disaster from happening. OR No, the South Fork Hunting and Fishing Club should not have paid for the clean up costs, as it probably would have bankrupted the Club. The Club did not deliberately cause the dam to break; too much rain did that. Also, the Club's president tried to warn the people in Johnstown with a telegram as soon as he knew the disaster was going to happen.

page 77

1. b 2. d 3. c

4. True. The fire burned everything inside the brick buildings. It also left the inside and outside walls blackened and smelling bad. In some places the flames were so hot that the bricks even cracked.

5. E. E. Schmitz was the mayor of San Francisco. He wanted people to stay indoors at night to keep law-abiding citizens safe. He had given the order for police and federal troops to shoot to kill anyone committing a crime. A mistake or stray bullets could cause an innocent person to be shot if he or she was outside after dark.

6. Yes, the mayor was wise to authorize the killing of anyone caught committing a crime after the disaster because it was the fastest way to restore order. The important things were rescuing people who were trapped, getting help for the wounded, and food and shelter for the homeless. Robbers take manpower away from the important issues after a disaster. OR No, the mayor should not have authorized the killing of anyone caught committing a crime after the disaster because there's too much of a chance that mistakes and stray bullets could end up killing innocent people. What if someone was climbing through the window of his or her own home and was shot for doing so? Also, I do not believe it is really a crime if starving people break into grocery stores or other homes searching for food.

page 81

1. b   2. b   3. a

4. True. The Irish ships that were to escort the *Lusitania* did not meet the ship, probably because German subs had recently sunk hundreds of merchant ships in that area. The Irish ship captains knew that it was an unsafe area in which to wait around to escort a vessel.

5. The purpose of the notice that the German ambassador had printed in the *New York Times* was to warn travelers that they were at risk because they would be on a ship flying a flag that German subs were firing at. The ambassador thought that if the ship was sunk, he had given passengers fair warning.

6. Yes, the notice in the *New York Times* was a clear enough civilian warning to justify the attack. The people who chose to go on the *Lusitania* knew they were taking their lives in their hands. The notice made it very clear that there was a good chance the ship would be fired upon by a German sub. People who disregarded the notice knew that they were taking a big risk. OR No, the notice in the *New York Times* cannot justify the attack. There was no excuse for the Germans to fire on a passenger ship, no matter what flag it was flying. The people aboard were innocent victims, not troops.

page 84

1. c   2. b   3. c

4. False. Hurricane Katrina formed in the Caribbean Sea. OR False. Hurricane Katrina grew stronger as it crossed the Gulf of Mexico.

5. Between 2001 and 2005, the year 2005 had the most strong hurricanes, and Hurricane Katrina was one of them.

6. Yes, New Orleans should have been rebuilt. People love the city, there are many historical buildings, and it is a popular tourist destination, especially around Mardi Gras time. OR No, New Orleans should not have been rebuilt. Since it is below sea level, it is just a matter of time before another huge hurricane will cause the city to be flooded again.

page 87

1. d   2. c   3. b

4. True. The British troops holding Philadelphia did not have the food, warm clothing, and ammunition that they needed because the troops at Fort Mifflin stopped the British supply ships.

5. The moat was an extra safety measure to keep the fort from being invaded. Enemy troops approaching from the river would have to cross the moat under fire from within the fort.

6. Yes, it was wise to build Fort Mifflin with its interior below the river level because then the fort's walls were not sticking up really high and providing good targets for the ship's cannons. OR No, it was not wise to build Fort Mifflin with its interior below the river level because the fort had problems with flooding and sewage backing up into it. This caused the men to become ill.

page 90

1. c   2. b   3. a

4. True. For every man killed in battle, another ten died of disease.

5. Great Britain felt confident that it could win the war since it had more soldiers, experienced military leaders, a strong navy, and the factories and funds to make the necessary war supplies. The colonists, on the other hand, had few soldiers, and they were untrained. They had inexperienced military leaders, no navy, little funding, and no factories to make the necessary war supplies. To the British, the war at first looked as if it would be as easy as taking candy from a baby.

6. Student must state one of the British disadvantages and give a reason why it's the worst. Student must also state one of the colonist disadvantages and give a reason why it's the worst.

page 93

1. b   2. a   3. d

4. True. Before the trip Lewis spent $2,500. During the trip he used a letter of credit that President Jefferson gave to him. Lewis ran up a bill of $39,000. That adds up to $41,500.

5. Lewis bought $696 worth of Indian gifts, which was the most expensive item on the list. The second most expensive item was the $430 he spent on horses and the materials used to build the keelboats.

Answer Key (Cont.)

6. Yes, Lewis spent enough money on food to take on the trip because there was a limit to the amount of food that the group could carry. The men expected to hunt and find plants along the way to supplement the food they took with them. Also, they thought they would be gone for just 18 months and ended up being gone for more than 2 years. OR No, Lewis did not spend enough money on food to take on the trip because the group practically starved going over the Rocky Mountains. Food was not one of the largest expenses on the list, but it should have been. The $87 he spent on "incidentals" (odds and ends) should've been spent on more provisions.

page 96

1. d   2. c   3. b

4. False. The U.S. paid Spain $20 million for Guam, Puerto Rico, and the Philippines.

5. No, Lt. Blow does not suspect the Spanish. In his letter, he writes, "their actions, sympathy, and assistance indicate that they are ignorant of the cause." He also states that if he is taken prisoner, "we are sure to receive good treatment on account of the sympathy of the people."

6. I believe that the Spanish blew up the ship. They did not like the fact that the Americans sent a warship to Havana to intimidate them. Also, the captain received a note from Spanish people saying that the ship would be destroyed. OR I believe that the Cuban rebels destroyed the ship to bring on a war. They hoped that American troops would chase the Spanish out of their nation. They thought that if the Americans won, that the U.S. would set them free because they were sympathetic to the rebels' cause. OR I believe that it was an overheated boiler or coal bunker, especially since similar ships made at that time had such problems. OR I believe that William Randolph Hearst had a bomb planted on the ship. He wanted the two countries to go to war so that he would sell more newspapers. It is very suspicious that he sent a reporter there to cover a war that wasn't even close to happening when he went. The fact that he said, "I'll furnish the war" is shocking and makes him sound guilty.

page 99

1. c   2. b   3. a

4. True. McKinley was shot at a party on September 6, 1901 (the day after the speech). He died on September 14, 1901 from an infected wound.

5. The magazine cover would help President Roosevelt's public support because he's showing respect for the dead President McKinley. If he had ignored the former president's funeral, people would have seen him as uncaring, or worse, as glad that the president died so that he had a chance to take over.

6. Yes, President McKinley would have approved of his assassin's execution because the death penalty should be used when someone murders a president in order to prevent more people from trying to do so. OR No, President McKinley would not have approved of his assassin's execution because the death penalty is a violent punishment. When the crowd grabbed Czolgosz, McKinley said, "Don't let them hurt him." This shows that he did not believe in violence and didn't want the assassin hurt, let alone killed.

page 102

1. b   2. d   3. b

4. True. The Pennsylvania amendment for woman's suffrage failed. But a few years later a Constitutional amendment gave all U.S. women the right to vote.

5. Yes, the wounded soldier would give women the right to vote. The women on the battlefield are risking their lives to tend to the injured men who are grateful for their care. These men see that the women deserve the right to vote because they are not lesser citizens.

6. I'd prefer to see the Liberty Bell because it is more famous; it has seen more history; it is more inspiring, etc. OR I'd prefer to see the Justice Bell because I could actually touch it and even ring it; I think it was important in helping women achieve the right to vote; I wouldn't have to wait in a long line to see it, etc. (Allow reasonable responses)

page 105

1. d   2. d   3. a

4. True. The article says that 70,000 of the 110,000 relocated Japanese Americans moved to were U.S. citizens. That is more than half (actually 64 percent).

5. The storeowner put the sign stating "I Am An American" in his window because he wanted people to know that he was a U.S. citizen who loved his nation. He was not on Japan's side simply because he was of Japanese heritage. He hoped the sign would keep him from having his business taken away or from being sent to an internment camp.

6. If I had been a young Japanese American male living in an internment camp, I would have volunteered to fight because I am patriotic and would want to help my nation win the war. Even if I was angry at the government for its mistreatment of me, I wouldn't have wanted the U.S. to lose the war! Also, volunteering would be a good way to escape from the camp and get to see some of the world. OR If I had been a young Japanese American male living in an internment camp, I would not have volunteered to because the U.S. government had trampled on my civil rights. I would have been angry at the government's not wanting to do anything to help them.